FORTY YEARS
of INVESTOR
MISTAKES

T0165730

FORTY YEARS
of INVESTOR
MISTAKES

**A FINANCIAL ADVISOR'S GUIDE
to AVOIDING PITFALLS**

BILL RILEY

Published by Advantage, Charleston, South Carolina.
Member of Advantage Media Group.

ADVANTAGE is a registered trademark and the Advantage colophon is a trademark of Advantage Media Group, Inc.

Printed in the United States of America.

ISBN: 978-1-59932-443-2
LCCN: 2014939752

Book design by Amy Ropp.

This publication is designed to provide accurate and authoritative information in regard to the subject matter covered. It is sold with the understanding that the publisher is not engaged in rendering legal, accounting, or other professional services. If legal advice or other expert assistance is required, the services of a competent professional person should be sought.

Advantage Media Group is proud to be a part of the Tree Neutral® program. Tree Neutral offsets the number of trees consumed in the production and printing of this book by taking proactive steps such as planting trees in direct proportion to the number of trees used to print books. To learn more about Tree Neutral, please visit www.treeneutral.com. To learn more about Advantage's commitment to being a responsible steward of the environment, please visit www.advantagefamily.com/green

Advantage Media Group is a publisher of business, self-improvement, and professional development books and online learning. We help entrepreneurs, business leaders, and professionals share their Stories, Passion, and Knowledge to help others Learn & Grow. Do you have a manuscript or book idea that you would like us to consider for publishing? Please visit advantagefamily.com or call 1.866.775.1696.

DISCLAIMER:

All investing involves risks and costs. Your advisor can provide you with information about the risks and costs associated with specific programs. No investment strategy (including asset allocation and diversification strategies) can ensure peace of mind, assure profit, or protect against loss.

This book is based on the views of Riley Wealth Management, LLC. Other persons may analyze investing from a different perspective. Nothing included herein is intended to infer that the approach to investing espoused in this book will assure any particular results.

CONTENTS

WHY THIS BOOK? — *9*

INTRODUCTION — *11*

CHAPTER ONE: Brave New World — *29*

CHAPTER TWO: What Lies Ahead? — *47*

CHAPTER THREE: Someone to Trust — *55*

CHAPTER FOUR: What Do You Have to Lose? — *73*

CHAPTER FIVE: Replacing That Paycheck — *87*

CHAPTER SIX: Threats to Your Wealth — *105*

CHAPTER SEVEN: Here's to Your Health — *119*

CHAPTER EIGHT: The Secret Life of Your 401(k) — *131*

CHAPTER NINE: In Your Footprints — *141*

CONCLUSION: A Good Night's Sleep — *153*

SUGGESTED READING LIST — *155*

APPENDIX 1 — *157*

APPENDIX 2 — *159*

APPENDIX 3 — *161*

ABOUT THE AUTHOR — *163*

WHY THIS BOOK?

People have always asked me why I don't write a book about my experiences gained from over 40 years in the public and personal financial management arenas. My purpose with this book is to help the reader to avoid some of the mistakes made in investing and financial management. The title of this book may perk interest because of the never-ending search for the silver bullet of investing. First of all, there are no silver bullets. Managing finances in this world of information overload is a daunting task even for us professionals. In fact, today, there is more misinformation than there is profitable information.

My objective is to dispel the myths of an industry in flux and explain why investors' behavior is the main cause of investment misgivings. You may relate to some of the investor stories, which are based on real-life experiences of some of my financial practice clients. Therefore, this book is more about what not to do, though it does include some basics on what to do. Since I view myself as more of a financial coach than an advisor/broker, we will be dealing with the psychological side of investing to a great extent. I have observed that until investors rid themselves of the fear, greed and gambling aspects of investing, their chance of success is very slim.

My career has been very good to me, not only from a financial standpoint but also from knowing that I have helped people move from the scarcity mode to the abundance mode, based on their current lifestyle. In fact, I am on a mission to work with those who to want educate themselves and discover the true purpose of money. I can help them alleviate the stress of investing by using academic theories and principles to obtain their financial goals. I can help them leave a legacy to their heirs and enjoy their life.

I have evolved into more of a financial/life coach, centering on life planning, not just financial planning. My message is that financial planning doesn't have to be stressful. Through the information contained in this book, and my workshops, you can experience the American dream. I hope you will enjoy this book and glean information you will find helpful in managing your portfolio and your life in general. This book should be just the beginning of your road to prosperity and it should help you realize that a well-trained advisor can and should be part of your team.

INTRODUCTION

By the luck of the draw, my number came up low in the first Vietnam draft lottery. My future seemed brighter, somehow, and it was time to sit down with my father for a talk.

Most people were ranchers on the north Texas range near Fort Worth. My father owned an aluminum and magnesium foundry and produced quality aircraft parts for the defense industry. During the Vietnam War the foundry was the primary producer for Bell Helicopter. It was high time for young Bill to make up his mind about what he wanted to do when he grew up. Would I join the family business?

I thought I could be a golfer and try out for the pro tour. I believed I was talented until I went out on some tournaments. That changed my mind rather quickly.

"Okay, Dad, I've got to make a decision about college. What do you want me to do here?" I figured that I could go to Texas Christian University (TCU), which was his alma mater, but maybe he would rather I went to the Colorado School of Mines, where a lot of the guys at the plant had gotten their degrees. I figured I could study metallurgy there, and I'd be a big help around the foundry.

He looked me square in the eyes. "No," he said. "I don't want you to do that. I'm a businessman, not a metallurgist. I can always hire those guys. What I want you to do is study business. I want you to learn about financial management—and about people. You should get a degree in that, and in psychology, because as long as you can manage money and manage people, you're going to be successful. That's what I do every day. I manage money and I manage people."

And so it was off to TCU, where, in three years, I graduated with a major in financial management and a minor in behavioral psychology. It was 1969. In the years since, I have come to see my father's wisdom. So much of what I have done in my career has involved developing relationships and understanding people's needs and motivations.

Dad was a hard-nosed businessman who was able to show me the value of the businesses that he and his associates were buying and selling. When they found a company they wanted to acquire, one that "fit into the mix of things," he would give me the responsibility of going out to look over the books and get an overview of the operations. He was trying to teach me how to analyze businesses.

Just as I was graduating, he wanted to take one of the companies public, so we went to New York to meet with E. F. Hutton. He bought me a couple business suits so I'd look professional. When we got to the New York Stock Exchange, he was asked if he would like to talk a walk out on the trading floor. "No, thanks," he said, "but my son will."

He was always encouraging me to manage money as a profession, and to buy and sell businesses. He didn't do so in a demanding way, but he tried to spark my interest. And it worked: I spent about five years working with my father.

Dad understood people. He died young—of a brain tumor at age 54—but not before he had profoundly influenced the course of my life. He knew I would have a hard time making it in the business world unless I knew what made people tick. *He* certainly knew. I would watch him at work and in meetings and I would see how he would get people to do things without being overbearing. He would challenge them. He called it "dangling the carrot." They'd get it done, and he had their loyalty.

We had a horse and cattle ranch south of town. My dad was interested in ranching and cutting horses. I shared that interest and worked on our ranch and others during my teen years. I steer roped and won a number of trophies. I snuck off and rode bulls for a while until I got caught. Dad explained to me the difference between a $50,000 cutting horse and a two-bit bull. I didn't get to do that anymore. But ranching and the horse business are still in my blood, and that's what I'll probably do someday when the time comes to slow down a bit, as it does for many of my clients.

Mistakes Aplenty

A major concern for people approaching retirement can be distilled into these words, "I made all this, and now I need to be able to hold onto it." People work hard to make their stockpile of money. When they come to me, they want to find out how long it will last—that is, whether it will outlast them—and how much income they can draw from it.

A lot of the mistakes people make as they plan for retirement come from having unrealistic expectations. They may fail to understand that once they get into retirement, they need to live on what they have accumulated. Their spending habits need to be based on that reality because they no longer have that full-time job to fall back on.

Other mistakes happen when people chase a higher return without understanding the risk involved. They often end up losing a lot of money in their quest for an ever better yield. And a lot of people who are heavily invested in bonds are in a lot of danger, as I will explain.

Since 1945 there has been a 5 to 10 percent correction every year. It's normal. As a friend of mine says, trees don't grow to heaven. If you're managing your portfolio correctly, you can actually take advantage of that correction cycle. But today, people are so anchored in the anxieties of 2008 that they get jumpy. "The market's going down; I've got to get out!" they say. They fret over some doom and gloom article they read, and their fear persists. It's really damaging. I see people come in with portfolios that have been holding cash and bonds since 2009.

Clearly, many people badly need an advisor to point out some very real risks they are facing. They lack a sound understanding of financial principles. In this book, my hope is to help people avoid those mistakes by getting a grip on what they need to know.

Learning to Accept Help

Managing risk is the name of the game, especially when you get into the retirement years. If you're a young executive knocking down $150,000 or $200,000 a year and you're in your 30s, sure, you can take some risks. But when you get to retirement and are trying to live off the pool of money you set aside, you need to manage that risk much more carefully.

A great many people who are sophisticated in their professions have wide gaps in their understanding of finances. I've told people in my seminars that there is no such thing as a sophisticated client, because, otherwise, they'd be running a hedge fund, not coming to me for advice. And yet the smarter they are, the greater their ego, it seems. A doctor might think he knows everything that ails the economy. A pilot might think he knows exactly when a stock will take flight or come in for a landing.

But when they hear what I teach them, rather than what someone tries to sell them, that ego tends to subside, as it must, if they are to become good investors. The market can humble you in a heartbeat. I see my job as helping people avoid dumb mistakes.

My client base ranges from people in their late 40s to nearly twice that age. My younger clients tend to be reasonably affluent people, often small-business owners who are starting to think about their retirement years and may be worried about what could happen to their portfolios. I also have clients in their 70s who still are working. I've worked with them for decades.

Some of these people retire and get bored after two years of playing golf. I help them look at investments and develop a second income, or a second career. Most have come out of a middle-management job or have sold a small business and want to do something else. I counsel them, and I help them analyze their situation to make sure they're not falling into a trap. Is it something that they truly want to do, considering the costs?

I also counsel people when they are selling a business or taking it public. A man might tell me his three-year plan is to retire and sell his business. I have connections and can help with structuring the business to get it ready to sell. I can introduce people to associates who are quite accomplished at putting such deals together. Basically, it's about monetizing a lifetime's work.

My ideal clients are people who realize that trying to invest money is not an easy job. It takes a lot of training. They want help. There is a more to investing in today's world than ever before. The pace is much faster, and once people tame their egos, they see the importance of deferring to experience.

My new clients get some homework and reading to do so that they understand how we will be working together. I want my clients to stay engaged but feel confident in my decisions. I've made my share of mistakes, I tell them, and if I see clients making one, I will let them know and expect them to pay attention. Failing to do so, I explain, is like ignoring the doctor when he says you need medicine for high cholesterol. Do they think they know better?

My clients have had prosperous careers and good educations. They built businesses. They know what they know. They understand what it takes to drill an oil well, but they concede they need me when it comes to understanding the market.

These men and women, for many years, have understood the concept of delegation. They know how to run a company. They have attended to the big picture and allowed others to specialize in the multitude of tasks that no single person can do alone. They conducted the orchestra. They might not have been able to play the violin, but the concert violinist cannot perform without the conductor.

If they understood how to delegate during their careers, then why not with their finances? They're still in charge of their money, even when they assign others to manage it. I tell people, up front, that I don't know it all, but at least I know where to get the information and figure it out. I want them to see that I have more experience than they are likely to have, unless they've done this for 12 or 14 hours a day for the last forty years or so.

Some Simple Rules

In this book, I will be emphasizing some of the simple rules of investing. Don't get me wrong. It's not easy, mainly because it requires discipline. Not everyone has the knowledge, temperament or inclination for investment, particularly retirees who often are eager for the many other pursuits they have been dreaming about for so long. But there are some basic rules, and if people would just pay attention to them, they wouldn't get themselves into situations such as the 42 percent losses that many experienced in 2008.

One rule in this new economy is that you have to diversify. We have to take a worldview. You need to spread out your money to the free market areas of the world. Another rule is that you must discipline yourself to rebalancing, and be strict about it. That's the key. The principle is fundamental: Buy low, sell high. The reverse doesn't work. You will run out of money quickly. Instead, when you rebalance properly, you take profits when you must and you force yourself to buy what is down, in keeping with your investment model.

Those rules work. Follow them, and you will come out all right. Sure, you may not beat the market every year. Some markets will run away from you, but if you buy as prices fall and sell as they rise, you will make money. I've never found another way to do that. Business magnate Warren Buffett is a great teacher of that principle. He buys deep value and looks three to five years ahead, far beyond the next financial statement. Unfortunately, most people won't rebalance their portfolios unless they have an advisor pointing out just what they need to do and when.

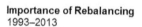

Importance of Rebalancing
1993–2013

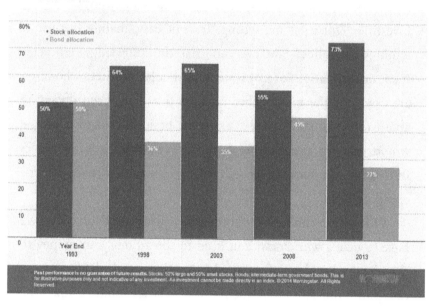

In this book I won't be offering advice on which equities to buy or sell. That advice changes by the season. Rather, I will be offering advice on what makes sense in your timeframe: when you should buy or sell and how you should allocate your money. We easily forget the basics and to do so when managing retirement funds could wreak havoc on our lifestyle.

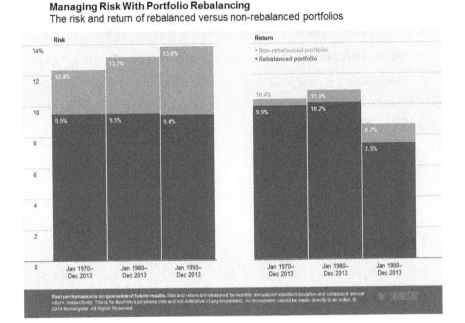

Managing Risk With Portfolio Rebalancing
The risk and return of rebalanced versus non-rebalanced portfolios

Treating People Right

I've been in the financial advisory business for 40 years, and I founded my current firm, Riley Wealth Management, LLC, in 2008. We're based in Fort Worth but have a satellite office in West Texas, at Graham.

For years, when I was involved in upper level management in very large firms, I saw that clients were not being treated as they should have been. The advice given them benefited the firm, not the clients. A lot of behind-the-scenes politics goes into developing products that are better for the company than the client. My company was founded right before the market crashed, but we didn't lose any clients as a result. In fact, my clients moved with me.

A lot of people like me have seen such problems in the industry and are trying to change some of the standards. Our firm, I believe, has a particularly strong culture of caring. I will help anybody, especially referrals, even if they don't have enough money to meet our minimum. My goal is to help people get out of that scarcity mode that has been so prevalent and get into an abundance mode. Even though a client might have only $50,000, that $50,000 is just as important to him or her as $5 million is to another.

Lifestyle Planning

My emphasis is on behavioral finance, and that truly differentiates my firm. It is evidenced in a 22-part questionnaire that I ask prospects to complete. It gauges what they know about the markets and reveals their mindset and how much risk they really can take. We show them what would happen to their portfolio in various economic scenarios. They get a real worldview and will see whether they honestly can take it.

A lot of advisors out there, particularly brokers, are trying to regain their footing and show how they beat the market in tough times. Well, if the market was down 41 percent and you were only down 31 percent, that's little comfort. We don't try to beat markets here. We determine how much you need to have your desired lifestyle. We call it lifestyle planning.

Market averages are fun to look at. "Wow, check out the Dow, it's up 20 percent for the year!" When excited people tell me that, I counter with "Do you know how much risk there is in that market right now? It's great that it's up, but at some point it will correct to the historic average."

We try instead to get people to adopt a reasonable mindset and expectations. They need to decide how much money they can comfortably live on. We can run an analysis on our software and show them how long their money would last at a given rate of return and a given lifestyle. Once we do that, a lot of people decide to delay their retirement. They realize that they don't yet have the kind of money to support the lifestyle to which they are accustomed.

They have to define that lifestyle before they will know whether they can meet it. It may be more extravagant than the money they have put aside can support. To pursue that lifestyle might require a level of risk that they would not be willing to tolerate or would not be wise to tolerate. In that case, they may need to work awhile longer. Or they might be pleasantly surprised to find that they can afford more than they thought.

Managing the money and setting up a portfolio is the easiest part of my job. I've done it for so long. I can make pretty good money for people, with risk-adjusted returns. What's harder is getting them to accept the fact that they have a limited amount of money and they have to make it last. If you think you're ready to retire and you have a million dollars and want to make that produce $100,000 a year, that's going to be tough, really tough.

My mission now, as I build my firm for the young people who work with me, is to get my message out. I feel sad when someone is referred to me for help and I look at his or her accounts and have to say, "I'm sorry. You have to cut back your lifestyle." If that person had come to me 10 years earlier, that likely would not have been necessary.

Sometimes, even the uninformed can ride the tide and do well, but we have seen clearly over the last several years how being uninformed can be deadly for your finances. I want to treat people right and give them the advice they need while there still is time.

A Plan That Custom Fits

I have created an array of financial planning models, 17 in all, and some combination of them will fit most client's needs, though we still customize the plan to just what the client wants. For example, several years ago I asked a couple who have been clients of mine for years—and good friends—"What would be your biggest dream right now?" They had worked together in a business and were highly creative and making good money. They said, "One thing we've always wanted is a nice home or a condo or whatever in either Jamaica or Belize." I said, "Let's put that into the plan. Let's take some of the money and put it into what we'll call the *Shangri La* or something. Let's start investing for that."

Last year they found a place. They sent me the pictures and the asking price and asked what I thought. Of course, I didn't know much about real estate down in the Caribbean, but I said it would fit right into what they wanted to do and they had the cash to pay for it. They tell people about that. "Bill asked us what our dream was," they say, "and he got us there."

I do believe that we were meant to live abundantly. We are made to dream. In fact, we must dream. We must set our goals clearly, because it's not until we can envision a goal that we can hope to reach it. If we don't know where we are going, how are we going to get there? That's why most of us need a plan so we can stay on track, and it needs to be tailor-made to our specific circumstances. It's normal to get off track a bit, and we need to make adjustments to our course.

GPS guidance has been a big help to me. I can just plug in the address, and the "young lady" tells me what to do, turn by turn. I don't have to think about where the next exit is. She sets me straight before I even start out, and she doesn't let me go far in the wrong direction without rerouting me.

That's why I ask new clients, "What's the true purpose of your money?" It often takes them awhile to answer me. They might have two or three million dollars, and I say, "You're fixing to retire. What is your true purpose for this money? You need to figure that out before I can help you. Do you want to grow it? Do you need to live off it? Do you want to leave some to the kids? Will any go to charity? Until you determine that, I can't come up with something that will work."

Instead of those questions, the first thing asked by most advisors or brokers, particularly in one of the big institutions, is "How much money do you have?" You tell them the amount you're working with, and you hear, "Well, here are three really good funds that would just be perfect for you." That's not a good approach.

I find out first what you want to do. Then design an approach, come up with a few ideas, and see if it's something that you feel comfortable with. I have to understand your needs and goals. Otherwise, I could end up putting your money in a growth account when you need income instead.

I met recently with a man who had been referred to me by a good friend. I asked him to tell me a little bit about himself and what he hoped to do. He said he had a fair amount of money, which turned out to be a couple of hundred thousand dollars. It's one of our smaller accounts, but I really wanted to help the fellow.

"Where are you investing now?" I asked him. He told me the names of a few companies. "They've moved me to a service center somewhere way up North, and I don't have a broker anymore and I'm not getting any advice."

Here's a man in his 70s, in the latter part of his life, and he has nobody to turn to. He wasn't profitable to the wire houses anymore. He wasn't making them any money, so he was shuttled off to New Jersey or somewhere. And yet his $250,000 was just as important to him as $20 million would be to another. I get disgusted, sometimes, with our industry. I was happy to talk with him about opportunities for growing his money, or creating an income, or leaving a legacy. Again, what comes first is to find out the client's needs and wants.

It's Not Child's Play

This is not a how-to book. I'm not going to teach you how to invest. I have a collection of books that profess to do that, or suggest the next shiny object to chase, and they're pretty bad.

Instead, I offer this book as a way for you to see where you have been and where you are going. You may see something of yourself in these chapters. You may discover where you have been making mistakes, and you may recognize that you cannot go it alone. You need an advisor. You may have noticed that E-Trade finally fired the baby. That is the commercial that suggested trading was so easy that an infant in a crib could do it. E-Trade finally realized the commercial was sending the wrong message.

Investing is no child's play, and yet people get the perception that anyone can do it. They may come to believe they've discovered the secret by which they can manage their way to wealth. There are no secrets. There is no silver bullet. It requires a lot of hard work, and it requires that discipline to buy low and sell high. That's the one simple principle that somehow gets ignored by so many in their rush to riches.

I recently got a rash of calls about Tesla Motors, the electric carmaker at $174 a share. I told people that they were back in the mode of the dot-com days. To meet that price, the company would have to make 321,000 cars a year for the next five years, not the 21,000 it was producing. It takes earnings to meet price. Otherwise, it's reminiscent of the dot-com days and the bubble that burst. People got caught up in the tech boom. I lost clients when I refused to invest their money that way, knowing that if I did, they would end up mad at me.

If you are going to invest on your own, you need a big helping of common sense. You need to do your homework and study carefully. Most of my retired clients don't want to do that. They want to check in with me once in a while from the golf course or from the RV. It always seems to be 74 degrees where they are, while we're roasting here in Texas at 104.

A Retiree's Biggest Worry

"Will I have enough money to last the rest of my life?" In one form or another, I hear that question frequently. It's the biggest concern that my clients express to me.

People need to consider that question realistically. Don't surf up some formula on the Internet and plug your figures into it to decide whether you can retire. You have to factor in so many considerations, such as economic downturns and rising interest rates and inflation.

What I show my clients—and what I will show you in this book—is a strategy to put your money to work to produce a dependable and lifelong income. And we will put that strategy to the test with various scenarios that you could face and see how you and your portfolio would fare. For example, if interest rates climb back up to 5 percent or higher over the next three years, how will you be doing a decade from now? Inflation is a major factor in retirement planning that often is not given due consideration.

Monte Carlo Summary
Retire 60 High tax & Infl
Prepared for Luke and Jen Affluent
This *Monte Carlo Analysis* runs multiple simulations of your financial plan against future market conditions. The result of introducing random investment volatility to the analysis produces a range of values that demonstrates how changing investment markets may impact your future plans.

The table below shows an upside case, the median case, and a downside case from the 1000 trials.

Case	Percentile	Total Portfolio Assets
Upside (Outperform)	97.5	$22,948,416
Median (Moderate)	50.0	$12,239,425
Downside (Underperform)	2.5	$4,256,704

SUMMARY
Upside Case $22,948,416
Median Case $12,239,425
Downside Case $4,256,704
Probability of Success 100%

This Monte Carlo simulation is successful in 100% of the trials.

Portfolio Asset Comparison
The chart below illustrates an upside case (97.5 percentile), the median case (50 percentile), and a downside case (2.5 percentile) from the 1000 trials.

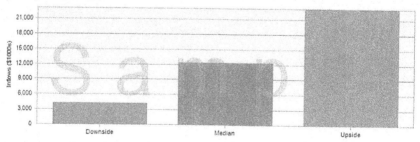

Onward with Confidence

In this book we also will be looking at other aspects of retirement planning. We will look at the profound effect of taxes and fees on your portfolio. We will examine the Social Security system and when you should begin drawing your benefit. Most people take it too early. We will address health-care and long-term-care costs.

Good planning allows you to move forward with confidence. It is critical that you work with an advisor who is firmly on your side, not just a broker who is working in the best interests of himself and his company. We will be looking at the difference between fee-based advisors and commission-based advisors and the type of fiduciary standards that they uphold.

You want and deserve someone who is obligated to keep your best interests always at the forefront. I work for a fee, meaning you hire me to take responsibility for your money. If your account goes down, so does my compensation. Only if I make money for you do I make any more for myself.

Stick to the principles that I will be showing you in the chapters ahead, and you should be all right. I want to help you move forward wisely and productively so that you can avoid the pitfalls and enjoy the fruits of retirement.

CHAPTER ONE

Brave New World

As baby boomers age, they are stepping to the edge of retirement in droves. Once they lose the security of that paycheck, they must depend, for the most part, on the power of their life savings to produce the income to support their desired lifestyle. Some launch into the retirement of their dreams. But many others are shocked to find they just haven't accumulated enough to live the way they would like.

I recently met with a client who told me how much income he would need in retirement to continue his lifestyle. I looked over his assets, did a quick analysis, and told him, "I'll be happy to work with you, but your expectations are way out of line. We need to sit down and really go through these numbers. You have a set amount of money here. For what you're wanting, we would have to grow your money between 15 and 20 percent a year, and that's just not going to happen."

I told him that before I could take him on as a client, he would need to understand that. "Otherwise," I said, "you'll be mad at me half the time." We laughed. "Tell me what I need to do," he said, and he agreed he would need to drive the same car a little longer and make a number of other concessions. He and his wife had a large home. "Have you thought about leasing it, or selling it," I asked, "or even doing a reverse mortgage?" After some counseling, he decided they didn't need that big house, which was completely paid off, and they would sell it. That raised some more money that I could invest to help him keep his lifestyle as close as possible to his target.

We all hate to make such decisions. Many of us keep putting off our retirement planning, thinking that we will have plenty of time. Then, all of a sudden, we wake up in a brave new world. We're 65 or 68 years old, and the time has come. We may not feel ready at all, what with job insecurities and business struggles. But it's time to take stock of the money we have managed to accumulate, and begin living within our means.

After that gentleman decided to sell his house, I also gave him a budget worksheet. That's something everyone should do when contemplating retirement. You need to get a grip on where your money is going. We have a software program that helps with that.

A longtime client of mine who retired about two years ago found that he had enough for retirement and for his golf passion. He's living his ideal lifestyle, even though he's a rather frugal guy. With advance counseling and budgeting, he was ready. He didn't have to back off his budget as much as he had thought. He just cut out a few trips. He calls me regularly, not so much to ask about his account—he knows after all these years that I'll do what needs to be done—but to let me know that it's a whole lot cooler where he's golfing than it is in Fort Worth. "It's 65 degrees this morning in Colorado Springs," he told me in his latest update.

And that's all right. I can take the heat, and I'm glad to hear he's keeping cool. As an advisor, I find it gratifying to know that I have helped my clients reach their goals. What saddens me are the times when people come in late. They have little recourse but to change the way they view life and their expectations for retirement. I can reassure them that they won't be eating cat food, but I have to tell them it won't work out quite the way they had hoped.

On the other hand, some people scrimp when they don't have to. They simply don't know what they can afford, and they are afraid. That's one more benefit of getting a good financial counselor who can reassure you when you are doing well and give you the confidence to enjoy the money you saved for so long.

One of my clients, a woman in her 70s, who has been with me for years, wants to leave her money to her children, but meanwhile, she is sacrificing her own comforts and needs, particularly with medical expenses. "You have plenty of money to do what you want to do," I told her. "Your house is paid off. Your income is almost what it was when you were working and you had a good paying job." But she keeps coming back to her fear that another 2008 could hit and she would run out of money.

I encounter people like that, who have accumulated some wealth but become very wary of spending any of it. It's good to be frugal, but within reason. People should enjoy life. Worrying about everything is no way to live. I have clients who have abundance but still live in scarcity, as if the world were coming to an end. But I also encounter the other extreme. People begin withdrawing far more than they had told me they would need. I have to lay it out for them. "The numbers don't lie," I say, "and unless we change this, here's how this will play out." When you have a plan but don't follow it, there are consequences.

How Do You Picture Retirement?

Long before you retire, you should take a close look at the kind of lifestyle you expect. How do you picture your retirement? I get a variety of responses when I pose that question. "Well, I want to travel," is a common one. "I want to play golf." "I want to spend more time with the kids and grandkids." Sometimes, people want to start a small business, or pursue a hobby. Some know they will need to work part-time to make ends meet. I've noticed that many of the workers at McDonald's and Wal-Mart are seniors. Others work because they want the satisfaction of keeping a hand in the career they long enjoyed, or they may volunteer their time to a favorite cause.

Many people become exceptionally busy, particularly early in retirement. They sacrificed for years as they accumulated money, and now they are eager to get out there and do what they dreamed of doing. They have no intention of sitting in a rocking chair and watching the world go by.

In fact, people sometimes that they really don't ever want to actually retire. "Well, you don't have to retire," I say, "just so long as you know your goals and the lifestyle you want. Why would you quit your job if you are happy doing it?

I ask small-business owners this hard question, "Why are you building this business? What's the end game here?" I often get this response: "Someday I will want to sell it so that I can retire." Then I'll ask, "What do you want to do during retirement? If you're going to put in 40 years to build a business and then decide to retire, have you ever thought about what you want to do? Are there any goals?" I help them to answer those questions and seldom do I hear that lounging on a porch is a major aspiration. Today's retirees are healthier and want to be active and enjoy life.

An Exciting, Troubling Time of Life

Retirement is a new phase of life. It's exciting, with new adventures to come and the freedom to pursue them, but it also can be troubling. A lot of people get depressed when they retire, sometimes, after a few years, when the novelty has worn off. I have seen clients who seem to have lost their identity. They were used to being the boss, flying to business meetings and going out to fine dinners with clients. And now what?

"Look," I tell people who are feeling that way, "find something you always wanted to do that you never did get to do, whether it's fishing or whatever. Get back into the mainstream and enjoy life. Don't just sit there. You have plenty of money. Don't lose your sense of adventure."

One of my clients always wanted to run a fishing lodge in Oregon. After he had been retired a couple of years, he said, "Bill, I think there's a little fishing lodge for sale up there." I looked at it for him, and we ran the cash flow for it. The owner was 80 years old and still working every day but wanted to retire.

My client decided he would take it on, and now he's loving life. He divides his time between there and Texas, and tells me, "This is the greatest thing I've ever done. I go up there to have fun even though it's running a business, and it's great." He had found something to replace the sense of loss he had from leaving his career.

People need to establish some goals not only when they're 40 years old but also as they enter retirement. You might want to work with charities. If you were an accomplished businessperson, you might want to mentor younger people on the art. That's what I would want to do—that is, if I ever retire. Your retirement can be filled with a variety of activities to pique your interests and help you to know that you still are contributing.

The prospect of no longer receiving that regular paycheck is what bothers many people embarking on retirement. That's where I believe that immediate annuities can play a big role. You can set up an annuity 10 years in advance and turn it on at retirement so that you have a guaranteed check every month. That's what some people want, most of all because that's what they long have had: a regular check coming in.

Retirees face an array of expenses much different from what they faced earlier in life. As they get older, they inevitably will pay a lot more for health care. I help people find Medicare supplements, but even with those supplements, the out-of-pocket cost right now for someone who retires at 65 and lives 20 years under Medicare can be as much as $300,000. People don't realize that. They need to budget for those costs and even set up a fund for them.

I had one client who called me at the age of 67 and said, "We're going to have to take some more money out of the account. I just got diagnosed. I've got cancer in my jaw." She and her husband were middle-income earners and didn't have a lot of money. I looked over her health benefits and their assets. The cancer had started spreading. She faced chemotherapy and hospital expenses, as well as traveling costs. They finally took her to see a cancer specialist in Oklahoma in an attempt to save her life. It didn't work out. Nonetheless, in only about six months, the out-of-pocket expenses were $20,000. This can happen. People need to face that possibility and be ready for it, and we counsel them on situations like that.

Such are the worries of retirees. Their concerns in life don't resemble those of young people just starting out or developing a career and raising a family. Retirees may have built up a nest egg, but the nest itself is smaller. After the kids leave home, that big house with the picket fence can feel mighty spacious.

I know that feeling. "There are rooms in this house that I haven't seen in a year," I told my wife one day. "Have you?"

"Only when the cleaning lady comes," she said. All our kids had moved out, and though they often visited and we enjoyed our time around the pool, we truly no longer needed the space, and the electric bills in Texas are mighty high in the summer. So we sold that house, right at the top of the market, in fact, before the crash, and we moved into a very comfortable townhome where everything was taken care of for us.

You kind of change your mindset. You go from the big home and that American dream to an attitude of "I don't want to mow that yard anymore." So someone else mows the lawn. You find a different lifestyle.

When you were younger, you were busy getting promotions and advancing in your career and trying to improve your lifestyle. You got regular pay raises and those raises tended to keep up with taxes and inflation to the point where you didn't worry a lot about them. Now, in retirement, you have no choice but to worry about them. They can erode your life savings if not managed carefully. You may be in a lower tax bracket, but you will still owe taxes and with rates now at historic lows, those taxes are likely to rise.

And inflation hits seniors harder than it hits younger people. If the price of a gallon of gas rises from $3.50 to $5, seniors simply have to cut back on their driving, whereas a young executive on an expense account can shrug for a while. When I was in my 20s, I drove a diesel Mercedes Benz, a great car that got me 50 miles for a 26-cent gallon of fuel. After a few years, the cost of diesel went up to 46 cents, so I sold it and bought a car that used gas—a lot of it. It was an easy adjustment, even if not my wisest one. But in retirement, the adjustments you need to make when the cost of living rises are likely to come right out of your budget and could affect your lifestyle.

I'll be bringing up the specter of inflation over and over in the pages ahead. I have to drive that point home to people, because failing to account for inflation is one of the biggest mistakes that people make.

Time Is No Longer on Your Side

When you are young, your biggest asset is time. In your investments, you can afford more aggressive assets and more risk. You get by during down periods in the market with the income from your job. The market has never been continuously on a down roll for 10 years, so when you are young you have time to recover from any losses.

When you get into your retirement years, however, you may not have a decade to wait. You may need your money right away. I see portfolios in which people still haven't recovered from the economic punch of 2008, and another hit like that would be devastating. A retiree's investment policy has to be much more conservative than a younger person's. As Mark Twain put it, "I am more concerned about the return *of* my money than the return *on* my money."

If you take excessive risk in your desire for a higher rate of return on your investments, you could end up having far fewer investments to earn any return at all. That's the way you need to look at it during retirement. Don't make the huge mistake of chasing some 10 percent return and designing a retirement lifestyle that way. You'll find websites that purport to help you figure out just what to do, and you can easily be led astray. You have to account for what a real return is. You must lower your risk profile in retirement, because you simply don't have all those catch-up years in front of you anymore. Time no longer is on your side.

As a wage earner, you probably contributed to your retirement plan every week, with every paycheck. For decades, as you built a career and a family, those contributions grew. Your portfolio expanded when the market flourished, and when the market corrected, you just figured you were getting a bargain for your investment dollar. With retirement far away, a down market posed an opportunity. That's the magic of dollar cost averaging. In retirement, however, that principle can work in reverse: No longer are you contributing regularly, but, instead, you are withdrawing regularly, and the consequences can be profound.

So Do You Have Enough To Retire?

"What's your biggest concern?" I ask seniors at seminars and talks, and the initial response invariably is "I'm worried that I might run out of money before I die." That's why, whenever I do a review or an update with clients, we first look at how their portfolio will fare under certain economic and spending conditions.

We need to find the right balance and the appropriate level of risk, one that recognizes the increasing need for a conservative stance but that doesn't lapse into paranoia. We have gone through years of deep market corrections, and I want my clients to see that they can get through times like that without long-term pain—and even with profits—if they stay invested with proper asset allocation and rebalancing.

Unfortunately, many retirees feel hung up on what has happened and want to keep their money tucked away in certificates of deposit and other such investments that are bringing them a negative return on their money. That's a concept that a lot of seniors just can't seem to grasp. They think, "I still have the money." True, but if gas goes to $5 a gallon and you're only getting 1 percent on your CD investment, the math isn't working in your favor. Inflation is stinging you. You need 3.5 percent just to break even, because that's the prevailing inflation rate.

Taxes too are a big detriment to investment portfolios. Mutual funds have been a big culprit. Most mutual funds aren't particularly designed to be tax neutral. Internal transactions create capital gains that can result in a tax obligation that could catch you unaware. There are ways to mitigate the tax bite. For example, exchange traded funds (ETFs) are much more tax efficient than a traditional mutual fund. Since trading is done with an index, not individual stocks, you have more control over taxable events, whereas with mutual funds, you lose control.

In deciding whether you are ready for retirement, you also need to assess your risk of long-term care. It's one of the hardest things for me to get people to do. There always seems to be an excuse. People often have little concept of how the need for long-term care could affect their portfolio.

If someone comes to me without a provision for long-term care, I will run the calculations. I'll say, "Let's say you're 68 now. You're in good health. All of a sudden, at age 72 or 75, you have to go to a nursing home. Today, in our area of Texas, the average cost is $125,000 a year. You might need a half a million dollars over a four-year period, and it could destroy your portfolio."

Long-term-care insurance is an expense that you must carefully consider. Once people do accept it and get it, they never give it up. Once they understand what's happening, they get it. If they've ever seen a loved one go into a nursing home and contributed to the costs, they are more likely to see the urgency of planning. I'll be going into considerably more detail about this, and about a number of alternatives, in Chapter Seven.

You need to have money set aside for emergencies and unanticipated expenses. It's important to have sufficient liquid assets available. I help people set up such accounts, and they have peace of mind from knowing they can, if necessary, access the money for health-care needs or other expenses that come up and that were not originally factored into the plan. That prevents them from spending down other accounts that might be fluctuating with the market, allowing those accounts to continue growing without interruption. An emergency fund provides a safety valve. However, you don't want to keep too much money liquid, or you will lose out on opportunities for a better return. Again, it's a balancing act, and it requires a close look at individual needs.

Another common concern that people voice as they wonder whether they have enough to retire is how much of their estate the government might take someday. I encounter clients who have a false sense of security in believing they won't ever need an estate plan because the federal tax exemption is currently high, at $5 million, or $10 million for a married couple. People think that is a lot of money, but if you save money and have a home and cars, you can hit that figure pretty quickly these days. Also, the payout value of your life insurance will be calculated into your estate, as well.

Estate planning is very much on people's minds as they get older. They want to know what they'll be leaving behind. Maybe one child has special needs while others are well set. How do you distribute the money fairly? Should it be distributed evenly or equitably? These can be tough decisions and should involve long conversations. In a lot of families, one child is highly successful while another flips burgers for a living. What's the right thing to do?

That's where a good trust comes in with a good attorney who knows how to put one together. You don't want to leave money without restrictions to a kid who isn't ready to handle it. He or she will spend it in a heartbeat. As a trustee for some of those funds, I find myself having to say no a lot. If you are passing on wealth, such controls from beyond the grave often are essential. You need to think through these matters and have a family meeting to make some tough discussions. Nobody is going to be perfectly happy, but at least when you pass away, nobody is trying to figure out what belongs to whom and who said what.

This is one of the more difficult sides of my business. People make a lot of mistakes. They procrastinate. They're in denial. A good financial coach will shepherd you through it, hopefully before tragedy strikes. We'll take a closer look at estate planning in Chapter Nine.

These are universal concerns and very much on the minds of most retirees. In this new stage of life, when people are moving from their accumulation years into their distribution years, I have helped many clients face these issues. They need a specialist to navigate these waters.

From Accumulation to Distribution

The accumulation of wealth isn't all that hard to accomplish for many people if they stay on track. They need a proper investment plan, and they need to stick with it. A good place to start is with a 401(k) retirement plan, particularly if their employer matches their contributions.

It's when people retire that things change. Their focus no longer is on gaining that wealth but on deploying that wealth as an income for the rest of their life. There are all kinds of ways they can live out of their portfolio. They must address their risk profile. They can't take bets or try to make up, all of a sudden, for what they didn't accumulate. Many people have gotten into worse shape by doing that.

Instead, retirees should be looking for an income stream, a check a month, as I call it. We can set up such a plan with certain instruments. We can run an analysis that determines how much income you will have to live on if you invest in a particular way. You won't be dipping into your principal unnecessarily.

The investment style is much different from a portfolio during the accumulation years. For the purpose of creating an income stream, I like dividend-paying stocks. A good one will rise in price and offset inflation most of the time. Bonds won't be appreciating, and when inflation rears again, it will damage a bond portfolio pretty quickly.

What Can Wreck Your Retirement Plan?

Dangers lurk out there, for sure, in your retirement years. The rules of life have changed. Even with a well-prepared plan, you must be ready for contingencies. A sudden illness or disability, a souring of the economy, the death of a spouse, even divorce—any of those can change your course dramatically.

One of the things we always ask people, especially upper-income people, is whether they have a disability plan. Social Security covers disability to an extent if you are under a certain income, but you may need considerably more coverage. A surgeon who loses a hand cannot practice anymore. An executive who has a stroke might be unable to carry on his duties. Just as with long-term-care insurance, this is a coverage to consider carefully. If your company offers it, take advantage of it. Don't think you are bulletproof and it couldn't happen to you. I always make it a point to be sure that my clients are aware of the consequences to their financial plan if they were to suffer a disability. I don't sell anybody anything. I just advise.

A stock market crash need not wreck a retirement plan, and yet people make big mistakes in their investments. They sell at the bottom and never get back in, when they should be doing the opposite. It's emotionally wrenching. But the worst thing they can do is get out of the game entirely and see the market return, as it did in 2009 and has done since. The train left the station, and many people weren't on it.

In investments for retirement, I generally look for the exposure to the market to be about 50 percent of the market risk, living with the fact that in the good years you will get 8 to 10 percent. The more risk you accept, the higher the return you can get, but the greater the losses. When you reduce the risk, your portfolio won't go up as much if the market rises, nor will it fall as far if the market drops. You can recover if your account is properly allocated and managed. I have some clients at a 25 percent exposure because their risk profile just couldn't take a 10 percent downturn. Our most conservative portfolio, which never goes beyond 25 percent, still averages a return of about 7 percent, and in 2008 was down only 5 percent.

I tell retirees that as long as they have capital, I can make them money in some way or fashion. Without it, there's no way I can do it. I can't pull a rabbit from a hat. There's no trick: You need capital, you need to protect it, and you need to get a fair return by controlling your level of risk and exposure to the market. Your best bet is to avoid dumb mistakes.

At times, we all are confronted by the unexpected. We all face emergencies. What we can predict is that the unpredictable will happen now and then, and it's a mistake to think we will be immune. When I create retirement plans, I show clients what would happen if a spouse were to die. Are the survivor's benefits sufficient? Divorce too can be tragic. People need financial counseling, particularly if a second marriage and children are involved. In Texas, the children of a previous marriage can make a claim to the estate unless the will is properly drafted. Texas judges sometimes will say, "Hey, those kids need the money. You don't."

Partly because of life's contingencies, you cannot always neatly divide the phases of accumulation and distribution. You may need to withdraw from your savings earlier than you expected, and your account has to grow even in retirement to keep up with inflation. The phases of your financial life will usually overlap, and you need elements of both no matter what your age.

There are growth accounts, and there are income accounts. If you try to get both from the same account, you can seriously compromise the growth. I call it walking on a two-by-four. You must be careful how these accounts are set up and these portfolios are managed, or you'll run out of money quicker than you might think.

The Do-It-Yourself Risk

People need a good financial advisor to help them sort it all out. In today's world, trying to do it on their own is probably one of the worst mistakes I see people make. They hope to avoid paying a fee, yet they don't understand the complexities of their tax situation, how much risk they're taking, and how markets work.

If you think you can manage your financial affairs on your own, first take a look at the 22 questions in the appendix. Those are the questions we address when we put together a portfolio. How much will be at risk? What is the asset allocation and how are assets correlated? These are matters that professional money managers consider.

You can't get the answers by listening to the talking heads on TV and searching for the hot stock of the week. Do you really want to sit in front of a computer screen and design your own portfolio or play the option markets or do you want to travel and have some fun? "I want to have fun," my clients tell me, "and let you worry about the rest."

After all these years in the business, it still bothers me to see the mistakes that people make, over and over. If they'd had some sound advice and used common sense, they wouldn't have made those mistakes. They don't know. They think they know. They think they can tap into all that online information and do without an advisor. You probably can find directions to heart surgery somewhere on the Internet, but I don't think you'd want to try it.

CHAPTER TWO

What Lies Ahead?

Years ago I worked with an optometrist. He'd been putting money away, and I'd been helping him plan for his retirement. Then he got the idea that he could start franchising his practice to other young optometrists to help them get started. They'd pay him a fee.

However, he didn't understand all the costs involved in starting a business. He started making early withdrawals on his retirement plan and paying the penalties on top of that, plus the taxes. By the time he got a grip on himself with my help, he had already spent half of his retirement funds, and he was 52 years old.

Other people fall victim to visions of grandeur, particularly after years of a really good market such as in the tech boom years. They come to believe the run-up will last forever, and they start spending accordingly. Suddenly, they find that their portfolios are wiped out, and they incur a lot of debt. Some file for bankruptcy.

Those who are far more likely to thrive in retirement are the ones who sit down and put together a plan, a guideline. It's always subject to change. It's not cast in stone, I tell my clients, but it does give them some boundaries. A wise retiree sets boundaries and has goals and priorities for the years ahead.

One of my clients was a top orthopedic surgeon who worked hard for 20 years. He would tell me about his goal of having a nice little chateau in a French town that he visited a lot. It was his retirement dream. Each time we reviewed his plan, he'd ask me, "How are we doing on the house in France?" Each time, I would show how much had been allocated toward that, until at one point I was able to tell him that three more years, at the same income, should get him his dream. "No one knows exactly, but we're on the way," I told him. We did it.

He's in France now, and I still stay in touch with him and give him advice on some of his finances. He refers other doctors in town to me. "Bill got me here," he tells them. "I'm loving it." Whenever he comes back to the States, he stops to see me. He told me he's working part-time and volunteering at a little hospital near his town. "I'm still a doctor," he said.

Those are the kinds of success stories that make an advisor feel good. He was diligent about asking the right questions of me. "Where are we? Are we on track? Do I need to do something else? Do you need me to save more money?" He had his goal clearly in mind.

Starting with the End Game

That's what I call starting at the end and working backward. Most plans start at the beginning and work forward. Instead, I want to know what the end game is, where you want to be. That's what you have to do when you put together a plan. This is a time to think carefully about what you always have wanted to do, what you will leave behind when you are gone, and how you will be remembered. What will be your legacy?

One of my clients learned that an animal shelter was running short of money and he wanted to help out. "That's easy," I told him. "Let's set up a charitable remainder trust. You deposit the money in there and you can start using that money to help the society. The society can only take the money out when it needs it. You're not just giving it money. Since you're the donor, you get to say what the money will be spent on." He's now so involved in that cause that he spends four or five days a week volunteering. He's retired, in a sense. "But not really," he says, "because I'm taking care of all these animals."

We all need goals, and an effective retirement fund will reflect them. I need to hear what my clients hope to accomplish so that I can plan effectively on their behalf. I may even help them identify some interests. Toward that end, we do budgets. Let's be realistic about the returns and stick to the budget, and within that framework the dreams can blossom.

Organizing Life Priorities

You have to know your priorities and specific needs in life before you can effectively plan any kind of retirement. The first of the 22 questions (in Appendix 2) that we always ask new clients concerns the true purpose of their money so we can help them decide on the investment portfolio that meets their goals.

That can be a hard question. You need to decide what you want to do with the money you've accumulated or are trying to accumulate. Are you going to grow it? Are you going to need income out of it? Are you planning on leaving it to someone, or do you have some dream or goal to fulfill? We'll see how we can work that out for you.

Once our clients have to write down the purpose of the money, they start thinking more long-term. If they want to get out of debt and pay off the house in 10 years, then we set up an account for that and they contribute to it. They know it's a long-term process and over a 10-year period, they have to stay in the game to meet that goal. I set the plan up as if it were a road map and my clients are taking various steps along the way to reach their destination. That puts people in the mindset of reaching for goals.

Financial planning has come a long way. When I worked at one of the big wire houses, I disliked the cookie-cutter planning they did for people. We just took the information, sent it off to New Jersey, and it would come back, and almost all the plans were, basically, the same. There was no customization, and no asking the hard questions about goals. Mainly it was a product sale.

As the profession has matured, so has the level of planning. The new Certified Financial Planners (CFPs) are helping clients to recognize that they will face specific needs and must adjust their plans for those needs. Perhaps a child has muscular dystrophy. Or an aging mother will move in with you. How are you going to accommodate that? The scenarios are complicated and cannot be addressed simply with "Here's what you need to retire, so have a wonderful life." There are so many variables.

Playing It Straight

To effectively organize your life goals and priorities, you need to develop a good relationship with your advisor. You need to play it straight. If your doctor asked you where it hurt, would you answer, "I'll let you figure that one out, Doc"?

With your financial advisor too you have to be able to open up and say, "Here are my concerns. Here are the things I may be facing." You may be worried about getting the kids through college. You may be facing the prospect of a divorce. Or you may wonder where to turn for help as your parents become older and frail. You must deal with those things in your plan. We go through a checklist with our clients to determine what we can do and how we can do it and what we cannot do.

What and who are important to you? That's one of our main questions. That's part of the true purpose of money. Will you be supporting charities? Whom do you wish to help? What do you want to learn?

A lot of people have travel ambitions. They dream of fine vacations, or they want to buy a home in the Caribbean.

We talk about the range of things that they could do in retirement. What are the first things they will want to do that they have postponed? And then I'll say, "You discussed all these problems. If I could sprinkle magic dust and fulfill all these, would you be happy?" Then I shut up and let them talk. That encourages them to weigh the priorities. Sure, they may want those things, but their primary concern might be what to do about an ailing parent.

Keeping It Real

Virtually every time, we need to assess whether the goals are realistic. Sometimes an advisor must tell a client, "Under your circumstances, you will not be able to get there from here. Your resources won't allow you to do that, and if you try, you will run out of money early."

We do calculations, mainly Monte Carlos on the "what ifs." What if you spent this much money? What if you do this? What if the market dropped? What if the market went up, inflation comes back? That way, clients can see the effects of these variables. It gets real.

If you have a million dollars and you come to me and you want to spend $100,000 on things you really don't need the first year, then you're only going to have $900,000 left. Is that going to provide you the lifestyle that you desire? You might have enjoyed that first year, but then you will have to settle for a lesser lifestyle from that time on.

Organizing Documents

In helping people get the necessary perspective on their retirement, we do a balance sheet with them and have them work up a budget. They need to gather all the documents and statements that will create a picture of their financial life, and we help them get those organized.

We have gone virtual on our system. We have an online "lock box" for each client, where we store all of his or her items securely on our server. We keep everything up to date. If the client needs something or loses a document, I have a copy that I can e-mail. I once had a client who lost his passport overseas and I was able to remedy that situation promptly. We've helped clients when they call to say, "I can't find Daddy's will."

Each client has a personal password for access to the lock box. Sometimes clients will give me that password in case something happens to them. You have to trust your advisor to do that, but a lot of people prefer it. We're ready for them in case they lose or forget something.

Besides wills and trust documents, we even store family pictures. One of the things I tell clients to do is take pictures of valuable items and we will store those pictures on our site. That gives people peace of mind that everything is being tracked, and the information is backed up daily.

Organization of documents can save your heirs a lot of time later on. I've helped clients try to figure out where everything is after someone dies, and it can be quite a struggle. My father-in-law used to take out a lot of insurance but never kept records, and after he died I found the major parts of them, but I found out about others through notification of lost assets. These were accounts he had set up or life insurance that had matured and the payments went to the estate because the insurance companies didn't know how to find him.

How Much Should You Share?

I tell my clients not to be too secretive about their finances. Otherwise, they could bequeath their heirs a lot of stress too, as they try to unravel their dealings. Organizing your finances not only brings peace of mind to you, but it's the kind thing to do for your family.

Likewise, all the advisors on your team who are dealing with your finances need to be regularly updated. A financial plan is like a chess game, with pieces moving throughout your life. You don't want to go into checkmate.

Once someone starts into estate planning, there is a point when the family and heirs should get together to discuss the plan, early in the game. It's always good to make certain there will be no questions about your intentions, even if some people might not like all of what they hear. This is a chance to prevent misinterpretations and forestall arguments. Remember, it's your money. You get to do with it what you want.

Then advise the adult children, as well. If they're going to get this large inheritance, they need some advice, such as, "Here's what you're going to be getting someday, and it comes with responsibility. Your daddy built this up, and I don't think he'd be very happy if you blew it in five years."

I'll be discussing that further in Chapter Nine, but in short, you may want to involve your family in your planning. You want to do everything you can to ensure that your final wishes are fulfilled.

CHAPTER THREE

Someone to Trust

Close your eyes and imagine the retirement of your dreams. Is it something like this? The alarm goes off and you lurch toward your laptop to check on your equities. As you sit hunched over the glow, your eyes blinking, you feel compelled to refresh the screen by the minute. Your blood pressure rises and falls with the market. Later, you settle in for a few hours of research to find out who's saying what, and it seems everyone is saying something different about what you should do.

To many, that would be more like the retirement of their nightmares. And yet it's not uncommon to hear from people that they want to handle their finances on their own. I ask them whether that's really how they want to spend their time and warn them that managing money is a professional pursuit. Do-it-yourselfers regularly make a multitude of mistakes. They don't know what they need to know, which can be costly, and when you are at retirement age, you may never be able to recover.

As an amateur, you're not privy to the research reports and other information that professional advisors receive daily. By the time important information that affects the market is generally available, it's often too late for many people to benefit because the stock price already has had its run. By the time you get the news, it seems everyone else is a step ahead of you.

I ask people who are considering managing their own assets if they have any idea how they would go about doing that. How many hours would they be willing to spend? If that's the lifestyle you want, if that's the kind of retirement you envision, you don't need me. There's no reason to continue the conversation. The reason you would be hiring me is that you want to have more freedom and be able to sleep at night and not be concerned about how some bankruptcy in Detroit affects your portfolio. I'm taking on that responsibility and that stress to find the best way to handle those situations.

I have the experience to know that there's nothing new in the market. History repeats itself. An event that catches you off guard and surprises you may be one that I've seen before and dealt with. I'm likely to know how to mitigate any damages. If you want to manage your portfolio effectively, you too will need that level of experience and knowledge so that you can take the steps to protect your life savings. Most people can't do that.

My profession is not for everyone. In the United States today, there are only about 340,000 registered investment advisors. There are a lot more brokers than that, but they don't do what I do. Look at the numbers. Only 340,000 people are actively practicing my profession, out of a U.S. population of well over 300 million. Obviously not everyone can do this. It's a lot more difficult than some think.

I also warn people not to think of this as a hobby. This is serious money. You've accumulated it. Don't treat wealth management like a hobby. You hear about the day traders and come across stories of people who made some money in the short term, but in the long term, most of them fail.

No Shortage of Bad Advice

There's no shortage of bad advice out there. Not all who profess to want to help you are really on your side or understand what you need.

Stockbrokers, for example, only gain if you take a risk. Traditionally, stockbrokers have received commissions. They get a commission when you buy and when you sell. In my early career, before we had fees, that's how we made our money. Some of those brokers were very credible, but I would sit beside guys who were big producers and whose goal every day was to make $5,000 or $10,000 in commissions. The clients seemed to be only a source of livelihood to them. If it came down to the end of the production month and they needed to make the mortgage payment, they would be sure to find some way to generate commissions, good or bad.

As a branch manager, I would see the production reports daily and as the end of the month neared, the trades would inevitably come flooding in. "So why did you do this?" I would ask, and the stockbrokers couldn't explain why the trade was good for the client. Most of the time, the answer amounted to "I needed the commission to make the BMW payment." Stockbrokers have a bad habit of living beyond their means. They are poor planners, living month to month on big paychecks. I never got into that trap. I was looking for lifelong clients, and that's why I started this firm.

In my early career, brokers were the primary source of advice. We were where the general public got their news. You didn't have all those talking heads on the business channels. People relied on their brokers. Sure, they had the *Wall Street Journal* and *Barron's*, but they didn't have the Internet overload of information.

Today, as I write this, you can do an online search for "mutual fund" and get 85 million pages of information. Who can hope to digest all that? I demonstrate that to new clients, sometimes, if they are still wondering whether they might go it alone. When they see it would take them decades to even get started on reading all that, they tend to get my point: They need someone who will help them make sense of it all.

I keep up with business and investment news so that I can serve my clients well when they come to me with something they heard on TV. Remember, by the time the news is broadcast, it has already been out for the institutional investors, and they've already made the trades. When the institutions start buying in, then we know something's up. When institutions are selling, you know something is going down.

Frustrated by the conflicting advice, individual investors may decide they're just as well off listening to a neighbor over the backyard fence or a coworker at the water cooler. And they get the same sort of mixed signals there too. Why? Because what works well for one person might be disastrous for another. Your circumstances are unique.

Platforms such as E-Trade and Scottrade run advertisements that purport to show how easy it is to trade. They'll show a guy with three screens and multiple charts. I have three screens on my table too, and I might have to add another one, but I understand what those charts are. I've yet to see a new client who had any idea what to do and when. Still, people buy these platforms. You buy the software and you have a black box with lights. Green means buy and red means get out. There's no light that tells you to get off the platform. Maybe there should be.

I actually do have a lot of respect for some of those TV commentators on the news services. A lot of them are smart people. But remember that when someone who says he or she is managing money gets on television, that person then becomes a journalist and, essentially, an entertainer. He or she might have a five-minute segment and have to come up with something, even though it may not be appropriate to a common investor. Again, nobody can give you sound advice unless that person knows your situation personally. Broadcasting is for the masses.

Many viewers figure someone who gets to be on TV must be an expert by definition, but some of those commentators got there because they look good and talk well and failed as stockbrokers. They have no idea who you are and what you are facing. I listened recently to one of the talk shows in which a 70-year-old lady called in and wanted to know if she should start investing in solar stocks. That would be a completely inappropriate choice in my firm.

Broadcasters abide by the fairness factor doctrine on balanced coverage. If you allot time for a bear to air his or her views, you need to allot a time for a bull to do so too. Through it all, people tend to just hear what they want to hear. If you're a bearish person, you're going to listen to the bear. If you're a bullish person, you're going to listen to the bull. Who's right?

The worst advice can be your own. Investors with the jitters make huge mistakes and trade at the wrong time, and people these days are trading far more frequently than they did 30 or 40 years ago. Trading in an account does not add much to the performance. Look at some of the great investors. When Warren Buffett buys something, he buys it cheap and holds on. He's looking ahead to what it's going to be worth in five years.

We had a new client who came in recently, and we started investing. "So why isn't my account up?" he asked not long afterward. "The market's up 16 percent, Why am I only up half that much? I had to explain, "Those gains that you see now were for people who invested last year, not right in the middle of an up market. Would you want me to buy high and sell low? You needed to have bought these stocks back when they were at a good price, not at their top. That's why you're still holding a lot of cash because it's a little dangerous to buy something when it's hitting all-time highs."

Not All Advisors Are Equal

All advisors are not equal. When you are meeting potential advisors for the first time, one thing you should ask is how they are paid. I bring the matter up during the first meeting because I want to make it clear from the start. I charge a fee that is a percentage of the portfolio. Because I am fee based rather than commission based, my pay goes down if your account goes down, and vice versa. Most people like it that way. It assures them that our interests are aligned. If you don't do well, I don't gain. When

I advise you to take an action, I am seeking either to protect your portfolio or to make more money for both of us.

The retail branch in a brokerage firm is a distribution branch, not an advice branch. Its job is to sell what the firms have put together or acquired, peddling it to the retail public. In the early 1990s when I was an assistant wire house manager, brokers jumped on the phone to sell what was called the focus stock of the week. Often, by the end of the week, they were calling clients again to apologize because the stock had lost value. And that's the way a retail brokerage works. A lot of people don't understand that. Brokers distribute what the wire house tells them to distribute.

As a registered investment advisor, I have to file an ADV form with the Securities and Exchange Commission. It describes our firm, our backgrounds, what we do here, how we charge our fees, assets under management, and more. It's on our website, and I encourage clients to read it.

If you walk into the retail branch of a brokerage, such as you might find in a strip shopping center, the people there don't have to file an ADV. They don't have to provide the full disclosure that I do. The difference is in fiduciary responsibility. A fiduciary must act in the best interest of the client. Our alignment comes down to the rules of investing often attributed to Warren Buffett: The first rule is never lose money, and the second is never forget the first rule.

We are true advisors. We are not order takers who get paid the same no matter what happens. I don't get bonuses or trips or anything of the sort. My fee is the same whether I put a home-builder index into an account or invest in Japan. My responsibility is purely to do the best thing for the client.

It's Quite an Education

That's why I get to know your needs and plans and strive to develop rapport and trust. We try to educate our clients. They get homework, and I want to see them do it. "What we don't want to happen," I tell them, "is for you to misunderstand what we do, and then, once we put your money to work, you call us, confused, telling us we must do this and we must do that, to the point where we have to do this meeting all over again." People appreciate that. They tell me that other advisors, particularly brokers, have never offered them educational materials.

If prospective clients come to us unprepared, we put them in a comfortable little office and ask them to watch a video for half an hour before we talk. I want them to understand how we manage money, our goals, and our perspectives. Sometimes it doesn't fit everybody. "I want to be more aggressive," a prospect might say. "Well, we don't really do aggressive," I respond. "I can refer you to somebody, but that's just not what we do."

A lot of our new people come from referrals and from our seminars and client dinners. "I want you to do what you did for John and Mary," they might say. "They really like your work." I explain that clients are different and then we go through the educational materials. Sometimes, I'll have clients who have been with me awhile and suddenly feel that they aren't making enough money. In that case, I might have to explain to them, "Well, you told me that you were going to be happy with 8 percent because you didn't want to take a lot of risk. That was a year ago when everybody was a little nervous about the markets. Now that the market's up, you tell me you are wanting to take on more risk."

Some investors go to competitors who don't understand the client. "I can do better than that," such advisors tell them. These investors are retirees, or they are nearing retirement, and the young brokers show them an aggressive platform of mutual funds that are all in equities. That's not appropriate for an investor who is trying to maintain capital.

Some of those investors didn't acquire enough during their working years to live the lifestyle they want. Even though they understand and accept what I tell them, when somebody comes along and says, "I can do better," they think, "Well, this way I could take those trips after all." I always tell people to be cautious about that. Brokers are only as good as their last trade. How much risk would I be taking in exchange for the prospect of such a return? That's the question to ask.

"If this guy is so good," I sometimes tell people, "I'll be happy to sit down and talk to him with you, and I may even want to hire him." That never happens, of course. They never come in. I say, "Ask him to show you some statements. He can black out the names so it's very anonymous and show you the results for investments he made over the past two or three years."

Anybody can go to Morning Star, pull up the best funds over the last few years, and say, "Here's what I would have you in." There is no crystal ball. What did well last year probably is doing worse this year. Hewlett Packard almost went bankrupt. It was the best-performing stock on the Dow. That's the way this game works. My approach is to offer trust and experience and show people, "Here's 40 years of how this portfolio performed." We have weathered a lot of storms and still done pretty well.

If you're 40 years old and making $300,000 a year, you could accept an aggressive portfolio. But most of my clients tell me, "Look, I see what you mean. If I can consistently make 8 percent to 10 percent and protect the downside, I'll win the race." They need only consider what happened to aggressive portfolios in 2008, or to people who were invested heavily in tech stocks when they crashed. That was quite an education for far too many people. I'd rather educate my clients before such sad events happen.

The Spirit of Coaching and Caring

A good advisor offers regular and consistent reviews. We set those up. My phone and my cell phone are open to my clients at all times. I have a good staff of people here whom they can call if they have some concerns. I always do midyear reviews and quarterly reviews depending on how much the client wants.

We emphasize the spirit of caring. I recently went to visit a long-time client in the nursing home. He's had a couple of strokes, and he wanted to set up a transfer if he were to die. He got teary eyed. He said, "I know, Bill, that you run a big operation, and I can't believe you made a personal visit to make sure I was okay and we were setting this up right."

I told him that I wanted him to feel as comfortable as possible in all ways. "Are you worried about your money right now?" I asked.

"Not in the least," he said. "I don't even look at it. I know you're taking care of it, and every time I need money, I've got it. I was always afraid I might be broke if this happened. I'm far from it." His gratitude touched me. That's the reason a good advisor gets into the business.

I make fairly regular visits to clients in nursing homes, and all of them are in nice ones. In fact, some of the best lunches I've ever had were at those places. You would think you were eating on a cruise ship. Those clients were able to get such quality long-term care because I had helped make sure they had the proper provisions.

In my firm I take care of 350 families. I say "families" because of the role I consider I have. I call myself a coach instead of an advisor now. I coach people through their lifestyle changes and manage their money properly. I only wish more people could find an advisor who truly acted in their best interest, but there are a lot more people who need that than advisors who offer that.

I love golfing. I was around Ben Hogan in my younger years, and Byron Nelson. I recently watched the guys in the British Open. Tiger Woods probably has one of the best swings in the game, yet he still has three or four coaches. He's likely to go down as one of the greatest golfers in history. So why would he need a coach?

It's a common story. The best athletes know they need coaching. They're not intimidated by the fact that someone is going to tell them how to do something. They have the raw talent, and they want to hone it.

When I meet potential clients, I interview them as much as they interview me. If I sense that a prospect is not coachable or has viewpoints that are far averse to mine, I'll say, "Look, I don't think this is going to work out for us. No hard feelings, of course, but we're never going to really be able to come to a meeting of the minds. Let me give you a couple of referrals."

My clients hire me for a service, and I must do regular reviews even if they think they're doing great. I still need to make sure we are on the same page and find out if we need to address any lifestyle changes. If they don't want me to do the job they hired me to do, they should do it themselves. If they think they can do the job better without any coaching, there's not much I can do to help them.

Successful people are coachable. Tiger Woods knew he had to change his swing plane because of that bad knee and leg. He got some advice. His father was his advisor when he was growing up, but his father eventually told him, "You need a real golf coach." That's how he got to where he is today. Edwin Land, inventor of the Polaroid camera, figured out that his strength was not in running a business. So he went to Harvard and said, in effect, "I need three good MBAs to run this company. Let me go in there and invent stuff."

Any good businessman knows that he doesn't know it all. You have to delegate responsibility. Many of my most successful clients here in Texas are in the energy business. They can almost sniff out the best place to drill an oil well. But they hire me to manage their money. They tell me they wouldn't have the nerve to do what I do any more than I would have the nerve to do what they do. There used to be an old boy who lived around here, a member of the Fort Worth Club. He's dead now, but in his early years, they'd take him out and say, "Where do you think we got oil?" and he'd go around licking rocks and say, "Here it is." True story. Oil men understand risk and do their best to reduce it by whatever means they have, I guess. I'd hate to think that anyone would lick rocks to find the best stocks for some amateur investors, though it sometimes amounts to that.

The Team Approach

I prefer the team approach with qualified specialists. I built a team with a certified financial planner on staff. I have more credentials than I need and a staff of people with all-around good training who give excellent service. We have two good CPAs to whom I refer people, and of course, they refer people to me. I have an attorney right next door who does a good job in trust and wills and estate planning. He gives some clients a discounted rate when I do most of the workup in advance, helping people figure out what they need and how to address issues. That way he doesn't spend his time trying to figure it out.

When emotions run high, my forte is helping people to stay in the game when they need to be there and to have the guts to pull out when they should. We take advantage of the down times in the economy. Longtime clients who have seen our performance and style of risk management will call us when the market is up to ask, "Hey, where are we taking the profits?" And when the market is down, they ask, "What looks good here? What are you buying?" Only a small percentage of American investors think that way. The others say, "It's down. Get me out," or "It's back up. Get me in."

It's up to a coach to point out why that's not a winning strategy. You should buy when you can get a deal. If you were purchasing a car and the dealer said you could get $5,000 off but only today, would you say, "No, I don't want that. I'll buy it tomorrow"? And yet investors commonly do what amounts to just that. A good planning team could help to steer them to the right decisions.

Estate attorneys regularly refer widows to us for planning services. Often those widows have never managed money before, and they are nervous. Even though we educate them, they're still nervous, because it's a difficult time in their lives. I will get calls such as, "I heard Greece is going down. Cyprus is going down!" I tell them Greece produces olives and yogurt and the country accounts for less than half of 1 percent of the world economy. "I don't really think there's going to be a major problem if they can't get it together," I say. But once Greece did start moving to straighten out its financial problems, some institutional investors started buying into it and made a lot of money.

That surprises many of those nervous types, but numbers don't lie. In fact, I open my seminars, sometimes, by saying, "We need to agree here before we get started that two plus two equals four." When people look at me oddly, I explain that if they disagree, then much of the seminar, in which I use a lot of graphs and numbers, just won't add up for them.

Ethics by the Numbers

The numbers indeed don't lie, but it is not uncommon to run into "advisors" who think they can make return-hungry investors believe that they can. Cases in point: the Bernie Madoff and Allen Stanford scandals.

When I was a UBS branch manager in 2002, you could select from certain money managers to help with your clients' accounts. The Madoff accounts were among those available. I looked at the returns and thought, "Wait a minute, how is this guy doing this? This isn't the '90s, man. There's no way this could work." Well, it didn't work. It was pretty simple to figure out. For it to take so long to catch up with him, he must have been paying somebody off. He was actually showing more volume than what was being traded that day. It was a true Ponzi scheme.

I explain to prospects that I use three top-quality custodians for funds: Raymond James, TD Ameritrade, and Charles Schwab. Depending on which platform I'm using and the best deal they give me, I can pass the savings on to you. I can't touch your money. There's no way I can get any money out of the account. Your statements come from them, and then we do the performance statements. You get two statements showing this is a Charles Schwab or a TD Ameritrade account.

What Madoff was doing was creating his own statements through his own broker/dealer in-house. If he had been using Charles Schwab, his scheme would have been identified immediately. Why his scheme got past the SEC, I don't know. I'll never figure that out. I get audited about every two years. The SEC has egg on its face. It was such a simple thing to figure out, and yet the commission missed it.

Stanford was actually selling CDs on a Caribbean bank, and he was getting yields way above what the U.S. banks offered. In fact, when I was managing at Raymond James, I talked to one of my brokers' clients, who showed me his Stanford financial investments.

"Wait a minute," I told him. "What do you think *these* are?" I pointed out the so-called CDs.

"They're CDs," he said.

"No. *CD* means "certificate of deposit." These are not FDIC insured. These are on Antigua Bank." He had over $5 million invested in them. He was determined that they were good investments.

I said, "Well, just call your local bank where you do your banking and ask them what they think of these. They're going to tell you these are not CDs. That's just a name." A nickname we all had in our industry was Allen CDs, in which the letters stood for "certificate of destruction."

There are still guys out there like that. I see Ponzi schemes because, as the compliance person for the firm, I get information from the SEC on guys who have gotten into trouble and what they did. That's why investors have to be careful. Audits now begin with what have become known as the Bernie Madoff questions. In my last regular audit, I heard them, right up front: "Do you produce your own statements?" and "Can you access your clients' money?" The auditor, almost apologetically, told me he had to ask those questions.

It's a matter of trust. Your statements should indicate that your account is held with someone you recognize and respect, not a firm you have never heard of. Everything we use in managing money is listed in the *Wall Street Journal*. Remember the old rule: If something seems too good to be true, back off.

The best thing to do if you're going to check out prospective advisors is to call the people through whom they are clearing their transactions, or call their custodian. I tell people to call Charles Schwab or TD Ameritrade to see what they think of our firm. As custodians, they have to do the research on us before they'll accept our accounts. They'll tell you the real truth.

Credentials and the Human Touch

Credentials, education and background are all very important, of course, and I need to keep on learning each year in order to keep my credentials, but there are other elements. There are people who have good credentials who are less than stellar advisors. There's something else, and it's called the human touch, the ability to work with people, intuition, creativity and a lot of other factors.

The credentials show that you can pass a test, that you had the discipline to sit down and learn and that you are competent. They do not mean that you're a good money manager or you can run a portfolio. Some things you can't learn in school. A lot of this business is pure experience and controlling your emotions and noticing things when they're out of kilter.

In the big firms, brokers are evaluated on how many assets they can accumulate and how many transactions they do. That's not even part of what I do. I don't look at how much money I can make off someone. I look to see how I can I help that person, and if I can make his or her account profit. It's not a case of, "Man, I have to get some more assets on the book or I'm going to get fired." That mentality results in bad decisions for the client. I've often thought that new brokers ought to be paid strictly on salary for five years to avoid that very prospect.

CHAPTER FOUR

What Do You Have to Lose?

I don't push my faith when talking to prospects because I think too many people try to acquire clients that way, as in "I'm a Christian. Invest with me!" I've seen more abuses there than you might believe.

But I remember my dad telling me the Bible story about the master who entrusted three servants with portions of his money. One guy just buried the money, while the others invested it. When the master came back, he was angry with the one who buried it. He'd blown his chances to do better.

He was like people who stuff their money in a mattress. Too many people do what amounts to just that. Even as we have been recovering from the recession, there is still $11 trillion "buried" out there that is not producing the investment return that it could. "If you are a Christian," I have told some clients, "why would that story be in the Bible unless we are supposed to profit?" If we have money, it is a gift from God, and we are supposed to be prudent and invest wisely. Otherwise, he wouldn't have given us that gift. Using it wisely doesn't mean giving it all away. It means investing it properly. To blow it or to hide it isn't a biblical principle.

A lot of my clients are what you might call the next-door millionaires. They live within their means. They built businesses. They took risks. They had the faith that they could do it and they became millionaires, but they didn't flaunt it.

I shy away when visited by someone—often a referral—who drives an expensive car he can't afford and wears a diamond-encrusted watch. My first thought is, "You don't need that; you're not a prudent investor." I think of Warren Buffett, who lives in the same home he bought 40 years ago and drives a used car.

My office is in Graham, Texas, where a lot of the ranchers and farmers have a greater net worth than the investors from the cities. To see them, you would never dream how affluent they are. They did the right thing. They invested, they took appropriate risk, they bought land, they raised cattle and they farmed. One client from West Texas owns all the little shopping centers in his area. "They came up for sale and it didn't get any cheaper, so I bought them," he said, and he's a millionaire. He's like many of my clients, with a net worth of about $5 million to $35 million. These are hard-working people who built substantial wealth, but to meet them you'd never know it.

Others think that the way to be wealthy is to spend money, live beyond their means, and drive the best car on the block. That's not how you get wealthy. You get wealthy through prudent investing with a willingness to take reasonable risk and accept good advice on managing your money. You get wealthy by getting started early in your investing and keeping at it. People in their 40s tell me they'll get started next year, and I say next year's going to come really fast. When I explain how much they will need to save each month to accumulate the wealth they want, they're incredulous. "I can't afford that," they say. But you have a choice. You can eat, drink and be merry now, or you can live well later.

So Much at Stake

A million dollars doesn't mean much anymore in retirement. It will produce income of perhaps $50,000 a year, and unless you live frugally and invest wisely and responsibly, a millionaire nest egg can be depleted quickly.

What happened to people in 2008? It wasn't really the American investor's fault. It was the fault of people who created instruments that didn't work. The public was led down a gilded path. There should have been more controls.

Much was at stake, and many took a major hit when the economy slumped. After we had come out of the tech wreck, the market kept going up. 2007 wasn't a bad year. People were trying to catch up from the losses they had taken in 2000, and they took too much risk. They didn't really see what was going on.

That was the best time to buy bonds. We lowered our equities down to about 25 percent of the portfolios, and we were able to lock in 5 and 6 percent bonds. Next thing you know, the Federal Reserve is cutting rates so fast that we're making 12 percent total return on the bonds.

In 2008 we only lost 3 percent in that portfolio. We still had a loss, but a really big hit to overcome is being down almost 42 percent. People weren't getting the right advice. They'd thought those trees would grow to heaven. The market never goes down all in one day. My technical charts had been showing alerts six months prior to that. Something was wrong, and institutions were bailing. Retail guys were buying. Later the market turned in the opposite direction. Only the institutional guys, like me, were actually getting our clients to buy back in 2009. Everyone wanted to sell us stocks. They said, "I want out, I want out."

When I spoke to a group recently, I was asked, "When do you think this will end?" I said, "Well, Ben Bernanke will decide; the Fed will decide." When? There are inklings when things are happening in the economy or about to happen. For example, back in 2008, people should have been asking why we were seeing an enormous amount of homes being sold to people who couldn't afford them. Why were the banks having problems? You hear rumors, and when things don't make sense, it's time to get out.

It's about Managing Risk

The biggest risk right now is missing a market. A lot of people have lost four years of gains. Good gains. It's going to be hard to catch up with that. We're not going to have another four years of 100 percent gains. You have to have a portion of your portfolio in equity at all times because you never can time it. You never know when the turn is coming. You can sense it, but you never can time it. If you miss it, you're not going to be able to maintain your lifestyle. The only thing that beats inflation, which will be coming back, is equities. Bonds do not beat inflation.

Wall Street wants you to take risks whether you win or not, of course, but you do need to have some allocation to equities if you are going to make it. Some advisors have been advocating investment in exchange traded funds, or ETFs, a good approach because you buy sectors that way. It's the stock pickers who tend to lose. When you buy sectors, your success ratio goes way up.

For the average investor without a coach, the rate of return has averaged about 3 percent a year, according to the Dalbar studies. Investors with good advisors and coaches get around 7 to 8 percent. Lately, however, as the market has boomed, most good advisors are lagging the average because they're risk managers. Some clients with good advisors complain that they're not meeting the benchmark.

Managing risk is at the heart of what I do. It's not about beating a benchmark. Everybody talks about what the Dow will do. I don't even look at it. I look at the S&P, the Russell, the Wilshire, and the New York Stock Exchange. The Dow is only 30 stocks. A lot of those shouldn't even be in there. It makes no sense to me why people focus on the Dow.

Dangers at Every Turn

The risks that any investor faces are many, and retirees must deal with their own set of concerns. People face the risk of a fluctuating market, the risk of high fees and taxes, the risk of becoming ill and even the risk of living too long. There are a lot of things that retirees have to think about that could keep them awake at night.

If you listen to the stockbrokers, dealing with the market seems like just a matter of buy and hold. If the market takes a slide, just wait it out, they will say, and it will come back. Buy-and-hold, for many years, was the discipline of choice, particularly before today's Internet information overload. Today it is becoming a dead discipline, though you still hear about it. Prospects tell me about their buy-and-hold strategy, and I ask, "How long-term are you?" They have various answers including "A year or two, perhaps." If you start investing, a complete business cycle takes about three to five years.

The problem is that the first time people have a down statement, they want to get out. Buy-and-hold also lets a stockbroker be lazy. Because of the advent of fee-based accounts, they don't want to really manage the accounts. They just want to set you up in something that would work out in the long run.

But things change. Certain sectors of the market get stronger than others. Buy-and-hold just hasn't worked that well. For example, people who proclaimed, "I'm a long-term holder" have made no money on Microsoft if they have stood by it over the last 10-year period.

Brokers on commission always get paid on a buy or a sell. They get paid if the stock price goes up. They get paid if it goes down. It's the investor who can lose, and if the loss is big enough, it can be hard to overcome.

Simple math makes that clear. If your portfolio is down 50 percent, you need a 100 percent return to get back to even. It surprises people when I do the math. I recently warned a client that two of the positions that he had insisted on keeping were never going to come back. They were, basically, what we call dead money. I said, "You're going to have to come back 80 percent, and that just won't happen. We might as well take our lumps. Let me put it into something that will at least give us some upside, because there is none left in these."

What does this do to your lifestyle and dreams? If you have a long-term bull market, the effects of buy-and-hold may be not as great. If you have a volatile market, which we've experienced these last years, buy-and-hold can catch you at a time when you have to withdraw the money you expected to hold for the long term. Your portfolio is down, yet you need the money for living expenses, and it's the worst time to withdraw it.

Most of today's investors cut their teeth in the long, unprecedented bull market that went from '82 to about 2000. They may be unrealistically holding onto the hope that we're going to have another 20 years of straight-up performance. They think they are going to get 8 percent to 10 percent or better. It doesn't really work out that way for typical investors, as that Dalbar study reveals. They get 3 percent.

When I present a seminar, I ask people, "Have you ever wondered why investment companies put the clause in there that says, 'Past performance is no guarantee of future performance?'" People try to chase the hot dot. The average investor just doesn't understand how markets work. He thinks, "Well, I'm going to hold this mutual fund forever." If you have bad years early on, however, the return might be accurate, but what happens to your portfolio is another matter entirely. You might never get back to even.

And it's not just getting back to even that counts. It's the opportunity cost of where you might have been if you had invested wisely and rebalanced in a disciplined manner, with a proper asset allocation.

Some people buy into the myth that they can withdraw 4 or 4.5 percent safely from their nest egg in retirement. That came from a time when investors used to be able to get 4.5 percent on a five-year bond. They could park part of their investments in bonds and meet their income needs. That's not a reflection of today's world.

When clients tell me, "Here is some money. Put it to work and I want 4 percent paid out to me every year," I caution that if the market is down 10 percent in a year and they take out 4 percent, then they will be down 14 percent. They will have that much less for future growth. That's how people run out of money. Instead, we work together to find out how much income they need and then put enough of what I call "payers" to work to meet that need. The rest can be left to grow.

If you're at 100 percent equity, sure, you could have a good year at 12 or 14 percent, but you also will have losing and under-performing years with the potential to quickly erode your capital, and I can't make money for you without capital.

True Diversification

Another myth that you hear from stockbrokers is that's you're going to be okay if you diversify, if you get a proper asset allocation mix of stocks and bonds. You balance them out, and if one goes down, the other will go up. People believe that. It really isn't the case because everything is at risk. Your entire portfolio is at risk.

But just what is diversification? As I write this, our main portfolio has over 12,400 stocks in it. They are all in indexes. We're finding the strongest parts and sectors of the market, allocating throughout the world and then rebalancing on a disciplined basis.

Diversification doesn't work that well. You'll stay in the game, but you won't get the returns you expect unless you rebalance.

Right now, we've seen some earnings reports come in that have been so good that the first time a company misses its projection by a penny, the price goes down. That's been happening with large-cap stocks. As I write this, we've started adding more to small caps over the last two or three weeks. We saw they were still underperforming. That's the migration of returns. People say, "If that's topped out, I've got to find something that's got some upside to it." Diversification, most brokers say, means, "I've got a little bit here and a little bit there. Let me throw some over there" with no design or purpose. It's a myth.

You need to be diversified over sectors and with some intelligence brought to the fore. And it's not diversification between equities and bonds. Bonds are not the world of safety. The riskiest class in the markets right now is bonds. People just don't realize we have had a 30-year bull run in bonds. This is unprecedented. We are into areas that even those of us who have been doing this for 40 years really don't understand. We have a feel for it because we've seen some of it, but we have no idea what the effects of this are going to be.

For most people who are nearing retirement or already in it and who are under age 75, I suggest 60 percent equities, 40 percent bonds right now. Now that gets away from the old rule of 100 in which you subtract your age from 100 and the result is how much you should have in equities. That doesn't work because bonds are now somewhat of a drag on the portfolio although you have to have them in there. If you ladder properly, as rates go up, you will take advantage of those rates. Chasing yield has lost more people money than the stock market ever has.

I still hear people saying, "Well, find me a 10-year muni or a 15-year muni." I reply that it doesn't matter. They aren't paying much anyway. Even though you think munis are safe, look what happened to Detroit. As rates go up, those munis will drop in price. Now if you hold them and they are insured, you will get your money back, but most people can't do that.

So I recommend a 60/40 ratio, or, if the investors are over 75 years of age, about 40/60. Where we are today with some of the lowest inflation we've seen in decades, if you don't have equities, you're going to get caught. Your portfolio will not grow. Nobody has ever grown a portfolio holding bonds. They've lived off the income, but they haven't had appreciation in value.

Now is the time. We ran a 40-year model, based on our 60/40 ratio model, through our Monte Carlo test and all the market gyrations—a thousand different lifetimes, as it's called. We averaged 8 percent with rebalancing. If stocks run up to 70 percent of the portfolio, you sell off 10 percentage points and buy bonds, whether you want to or not. That's adverse to most people. They want to buy what's up. But what's hot will inevitably cool.

True diversification is having money in every asset class out there, not just stocks and bonds. You may need some real estate in there if the timing is right. You may need some commodities in there if we get back into inflation. There will be some volatility, but they do need to be in there even though they are underperforming now in the portfolios. There are safe ways to play commodities, especially ETFs.

We're hyperdiversified. When you add these asset classes, you will get decent returns, and most of the time, our portfolios have only about half the risk of the market. We remind people of that when they tell us that a buddy's portfolio is performing at a couple percentage points higher than ours. Do they want to accept the risk that would come with getting that kind of money?

Even when the advisor is doing exactly what clients are asking when they say they want to protect their money and produce an income for retirement, they always compare the returns with others. I remind them that they told me what they wanted and that I managed their money accordingly. In return for a somewhat lower rate, they are less exposed to the possibility of losing their capital and taking hits from which they might never recover. Once you are in retirement, you cannot afford a hit.

The Market Never Forgets

Daily I run into people looking in their rear view mirror. They want to talk about the past: how the market took a hit, or whatever happened. But the market never forgets. It remembers to go up from time to time. Just look at a long-term chart. The market reflects what investors often forget. What they remember is that they lost money, or "My daddy never made money in the market." The market also falls, yes, but before and after each fall, it rises.

In 1929 the Dow was at 381, at its high point before the great crash. It bottomed at about 41 in the summer of '32. Look where it is now. People have to understand that despite downturns, opportunities await them if they manage and rebalance. There have been times we were not too heavy in equities, as when we went into 2008, because I made the call that something was drastically wrong, so we loaded up on bonds. Today, stocks have gone up and bonds have gone down. We have positioned ourselves well to get through that.

An investor needs to weigh the risk and consider the timeframe. If you need the money in six months, don't invest it. If you won't need it for three years, then you can see what you can do with a moderate portfolio.

You need more than savings accounts and CDs. Today, one- and two-year CDs are at 0.10 percent. People think CDs are safe. They are swallowed by inflation. But it's also folly to chase hot tips. I had guys call in wanting to buy Dell when it was at $700. I explained that was an all-time high and it needed to back off before we might consider it. You don't buy a stock when it is has gone that fast that quickly. If clients insist, I suggest they go elsewhere to trade and leave their safe money with me. In 40 years, I've never gotten trapped.

The history of the market over time shows true patterns. "Here are the technicals," I tell clients, and show them that a stock already has had its run, or that it's down and facing resistance. You need to know the flow of the money. That's how you judge when you can put your money into either individual stocks or sectors of the market.

Mind over Money

Warren Buffett recently commented that when his Berkshire Hathaway fund experienced pullbacks, down 50 percent four times since he started it, he just bought more and it worked out. He did what most people won't. He's rich, and they are not.

Jesse Livermore, the great Depression-era investor, said that the time to buy is when there is blood in the streets and then you sell it back when people figure out it's a good deal. That's what the pros do.

Investors need to practice mind over money. You've got to have a mental toughness to do what you must, despite the emotions involved.

Back when the U.S. government was allocating money under the Troubled Asset Relief Program, or TARP, the president of GM was asked if he would work for a dollar if the company got the loan. Sure, he said. The Ford executive, meanwhile, said he would not, and that he didn't need that money. We purchased Ford right away. "We have to go in, guys," I said. "There's something there."

That's mind over money: to be disciplined enough to say, "Obviously, there's something there" or "I know I don't want to do this." That's why disciplined rebalancing is so important because it forces you to do it. People tend to want to hold on to their winners so they can talk about it. But winners can turn into losers and losers into winners very fast. I always tell people that they don't have a profit when it is just on paper.

There are two major reasons for unwise investing. One is being foolhardy and going with the crowd, buying at the wrong time. The other one is being fearful and running scared. Those together are the mark of an amateurish investor. It isn't your fault if you're inexperienced. Most people are. The trick is to know when you lack experience and to get some professional advice. The hardest thing for me to get people to do is to get over their egos.

CHAPTER FIVE

Replacing That Paycheck

A client recently announced to me that he planned to retire at age 62. He was pleased with how we were managing his money and said that if he added his Social Security benefit, he could live just fine.

"Now wait a minute," I told him. "If you take it at 62, it will cost you up to a quarter of a million to $300,000 over your lifetime. Let me run you an analysis."

What we showed him through the software was all the different ways that a Social Security benefit can be managed and that nobody ever seems to explain. He had plenty of money for living expenses without Social Security, and waiting four years until he was 66 would increase his benefit by about 37 to 42 percent.

"I didn't know the way that worked. I thought you just got a flat fee," he said. People often misunderstand that. The amount of the benefit depends on how long you wait before you start taking it. If you elect to wait, you can always change your mind and apply if things go awry and you need the money. "But once you start it," I told him, "you can't stop it. It's locked in. Do you want to do that?"

We looked at some alternatives for him. He decided to go ahead with a deferred comp plan with the oil company. He purchased a fixed annuity to make up the difference from his Social Security for those years. That gave him the comfort of a monthly check. Through careful planning, he was able to make the most of his retirement funds to produce a dependable lifelong income.

An Income for a Lifetime

Unfortunately, most people don't plan. Some have come to me three months before they want to retire without having considered how to do it. They have no idea how much money they actually spend, what their discretionary expenses are, or how much they are going to need for health care and various other expenses.

I point out to them what should seem obvious: That paycheck will cease. No more bonuses. The overtime is over. You have to be disciplined about how you spend your money. I want my clients to enjoy life, but I don't want them to run out of money. They have to find the right investment balance to secure an income and also to offset inflation. Inflation won't hurt a salaried person that much. The boss knows he has to eventually offer a raise or lose the employee. In retirement, however, you don't have that buffer. Inflation can hit you right between the eyes.

Balancing income needs with lifestyle desires takes finesse. People need to reconcile their retirement desires with their lack of a salary. They may need coaching to understand the realities and the necessity of living within their means.

What they should do is focus on income streams. When I create a retirement portfolio, part of it is in growth and part is in income-generating instruments, such as dividend-paying stocks. How much is devoted to the latter depends on needs. The account should be conservative. It's great to say, "I was up 20 percent, 30 percent" when you're earning a salary, because you could survive if that were how much you were down. In retirement, your chances of recovery would be slim. Sometimes we have to adjust those portfolios drastically as we go from trying to appreciate capital to preserving capital. There are times in the market, such as in 2008, when you do that.

Still, people get a flier from a cruise line and want to spend $10,000 or $15,000 in the first year of retirement. I say, "That's wonderful, but let me show you what that does because you haven't given the portfolio enough time to accumulate those gains. What you should do is wait until you have excess returns, which you do, and then take it out, run an analysis, and make sure it's not going to hurt you." That's what I mean by a disciplined approach.

Instead of thinking about your nest *egg*, you should think about your nest *eggs*. Each of those eggs should have a separate purpose. If you want a house in Belize, or wherever, you need to dedicate an egg to that purpose and wait until it grows enough. Do it rationally rather than just saying, "I deserve this." It's your portfolio that will determine that.

We set up separate accounts, but then we also look at the totality of your assets and run them all together. If you pull this amount out for that purpose, what will the effect be 10 years from now? If you get that vacation home, will you have the money to fly there?

Three Competing Needs

A principle of investing is that you can position your money for three purposes, in a variety of combinations. You can have liquidity so that it is readily available; you can have safety, so that you need not worry about losing it; and you can have growth, so that the money grows enough to offset the rising costs of living and allows you to enhance your lifestyle.

The first thing I tell people when they get into retirement, or are nearing retirement, is that if they tie themselves up in some instrument or investment, they can't readily access those funds if they need them. The lack of liquidity could put them in a precarious situation. I'll give an example. You can buy what are called viatical settlements, in which people sell their insurance policies. You're with a group, and you all buy some guy out of his insurance, and when he dies, you divvy up the death benefits. The problem is that these companies have a hard time predicting when people will die.

I've had several people come to me with these investments. They can't get their money out until the death. They expect he's going to die in four years, and eight years later, they still have to contribute premium payments. I've seen instances in which people have put 60 to 70 percent of their portfolios in those things, and there is just no access to the money, no liquidity. And it's kind of morbid to go around hoping someone will die.

Safety is another very important element to financial planning. In retirement, your risk profile has to be moderated because there is no time to catch up in the case of a big pullback. Everything has risk. Even a CD has risk because it cannot keep up with inflation. A lot of an investment's safety comes from its level of liquidity. If you see something turning south, you want to be able get out of it quickly.

You need a reasonable amount of growth, but you must rein in your expectations. A big problem I often see is that retirees who lack enough money for their lifestyle believe they must make a 12 or 15 percent return. That isn't going to happen consistently. The market over the last 40 years has returned 7 or 8 percent a year on average, so you need to look closely at the risk level if someone promises 12 to 15 percent. How could it be possible? Bernie Madoff couldn't do it.

Nonetheless, if your investment isn't growing at about two times today's inflation rate, you will be hit hard when inflation does rear again. I'm not saying that if inflation gets back to 5 percent or 6 percent, you should be doing 12, but in today's world, you need to build in a cushion. Inflation not only diminishes your purchasing power but it also can deflate the stock market.

A sound retirement plan, therefore, must provide a good balance of safety so your income is guaranteed to have liquidity—you have accessible in emergencies—and growth so you can beat inflation, grow your portfolio to replenish income needs, and leave an inheritance.

In determining that balance, the key questions are these: How much do you need? How long will you need it? When can you start taking it? I help clients determine the income they will need for the rest of their lives to maintain their current lifestyle, bearing in mind that most people spend about 70 to 80 percent as much in retirement as they spend in their working years.

When you can begin withdrawing that money as income will depend on your needs and on what other reserves you have. I tell people to wait until they are required to make withdrawals on their IRAs, because anything they take out is taxed. With your other investments, sure, you pay taxes as you go, but those taxes are capital gains and interest, and they are nothing like the taxes on your retirement accounts. We try to put off paying those taxes as long as we can.

Meanwhile, we can set up a quality annuity program and wait 10 years before turning it on. We show people how much income an annuity program will produce. Think of your annuity as a tin can buried in the backyard so you can't get at it. Suppose you have two other cans that you can get to easily. For every dollar you put in one of them, you get back two; in the other, buried can, you get back three. Which can is likely to have more money after 10 years? Most people will spend the accessible money. You can think of an annuity that way. If you try to get at the money too soon, you will be penalized.

The right balance of liquidity, safety and growth is unique to each retiree. Everything should be customized. There are no cookie cutters in this business because you have to deal with people's emotions, needs, expectations, family matters, health matters, and more.

Social Security Insecurities

Within 10 years, more people may be on Social Security than

working, judging from the way the job market is right now. Ten thousand people a day are retiring, and that is inevitably going to put a lot of strain on the system.

Most of those retirees would be better off waiting before collecting their benefit. Those who retire at 62 often opt to take an early Social Security benefit. They may know that the benefit will be somewhat smaller if they take it early, but they don't realize that they're costing themselves perhaps $300,000 over a lifetime.

The risk of running out of money before dying is real. That is why you need to closely analyze your Social Security benefit. You might be quite surprised to learn how much you can extend your income or upgrade your lifestyle just by delaying the date when you start collecting your benefit.

Many ask whether they can depend on Social Security. I think that the benefit will be intact for people who are 55 years of age or older. Younger people could face a struggle. That's why I tell people to start their retirement planning early. I tell them, "What if Social Security is either reduced or it's not what you think it is? If you're relying on that, you'd better plan. You'd better put some money away in a 401(k) or whatever your company provides just in case this doesn't work out so well."

Our changing demographic could significantly influence the Social Security system. When we run a financial plan or an investment analysis for people, we show it to them both with and without Social Security. That isn't meant to suggest they won't get it, but we need to acknowledge that the rules could change. You might have to be 70 years old before collecting. And if, today, you are only 35 or 40 years old, don't count on Social Security being there for you.

I don't want to scare you. I have no qualms that mine will be there. My concern is for the generation under 55 years of age. Some of the money has been sequestered, and the government knows it has to pay it out. The question is how are young people going to keep it going? Wages have been low, and the investments on Social Security have to be in U.S. Treasury bonds, which have been getting next to nothing. It's going to be tricky. That's why I'm a big proponent of allowing young people to have some of the money in equities, even if government regulated.

In deciding when to take your Social Security benefit, you also need to consider the fact that a portion of your benefits is likely to be taxable. For example, right now, if you are single, you can earn $34,000, after which your benefit will begin to be taxed. If you're married, it's $44,000. That figure includes not only salaries but also, now, tax-free income and interest. That income "threshold" is based on a screwy formula that basically means you are paying back anywhere from 30 to 40 cents on the dollar of what you already paid taxes on. Those were your tax dollars that you put away, and now if your income is too high, you pay again. I think it's totally unfair.

When I explain this to people, that's when the conversation often turns to the possibility of delaying the Social Security benefit. I suggest to them that they delay it because they're not going to come out very well if they're taking their Social Security benefit and a third of it goes back to taxes. If a married couple makes more than $44,000, they run into that tax trap. A lot of my clients have investments that could kick out $120,000 or $130,000 a year, so I suggest waiting as long as they can.

I explain to my clients how to get the greatest advantage from the Social Security system. I produce comparative figures for people at differing income levels, particularly those still making over $110,000 a year. Often there's no reason to take the benefit early. You can make more money by holding off, and married couples perhaps can take advantage of each other's spousal benefits. There are techniques for managing the Social Security benefit that many people aren't aware of.

Filling the Income Gap

I have a client who started a company about 10 years ago and recently told me he wanted to retire in about five years. I ran calculations to determine what we could do in five years, based on his savings and on the market history and on what we know our portfolios have done in the past.

Unfortunately, I had to sit down with him and say, "Yeah. You can retire, but you can't retire with the lifestyle that you have now. What I need you to do is put more money away than you are now"—which he had trouble with because he had a nice life-style—"or you're going to have to work for 10 years."

He hadn't realized how much money he would need to retire with that lifestyle. He wanted $250,000 a year. If he had had $5 million and were to take out 5 percent a year, that's how much he would have had, but he was short of that and wouldn't sell the company.

A lot of people, of greater or lesser means, think they can just throw in the towel at 62 years of age and somehow manage to keep their lifestyle up. It doesn't work that way. The first thing I had to tell a lot of my clients was that there was no way they could retire at 62 or 64 years of age and keep their lifestyle. Some people keep working in some capacity or other—perhaps they continue to be very active in running a business—but a lot of people just want out of the trap. Unfortunately, they haven't saved enough to do that.

You have to create an income for retirement. The old formulas don't work. Pensions are largely a thing of the past. Very few people work for companies with a pension plan that comes close to resembling what their parents or grandparents had. Companies have turned the responsibility for retirement planning over to the employees themselves, via a 401(k) or similar plan, in which the employer might match contributions. But the days are over when you put 20 years into a big corporation, got your gold watch, and retired to collect a pension check. And as we have seen, Social Security is tenuous. For an income plan, you're depending on your own investments and your own savvy to a large extent.

In doing so, you need to think about those principles of liquidity, safety and growth. They are the building blocks for a retirement plan. In retirement, you need money for all three purposes, and unless you balance those properly, you're going to run into trouble somewhere along the line.

You can't guess when you can retire. You have to know. With our models and analysis, we can tell our clients whether they can retire comfortably at a target age, assuming they stay on track. If you want to retire at age 65 and lack sufficient money, we can talk about lifestyle changes to make it possible. You may have to sell the big house, maybe buy a cheaper car and cut out some expenses. You're no longer getting a salary, so this money has to last.

Every prospective retiree has, to some extent, what I call "the gap." That gap is the difference between how much money you need for retirement income and how much your investments will produce for you, beyond any guaranteed income sources such as a pension or Social Security.

How you fill that gap comes down to either cutting expenses or enhancing your savings and investments. Many people do both. Most people in today's world don't have enough in their 401(k) for the kind of retirement they want. A lot of the shortfall has been due to the market. A lot has been from job losses. And people have simply been reluctant to invest as much as they should.

I tell people who are preparing for retirement to get out of debt as much as possible. You don't need those big house and car payments. Be sure that your next car fits your budget, and at this stage of your life, does the size of your house still match your lifestyle? It might be time to sell and buy a smaller one or consider a reverse mortgage.

Your planning needs to include an assessment of how much money you need for your essential expenses, and how much you would need to meet your life goals. What are the necessities, and what would be the niceties? I ask my clients, "If you find that you have an abundance of money rather than a scarcity, and have money to spend in a good year without hurting your retirement plan, what would you like to do with it?" I get answers such as "take a trip to Europe" and "go fishing" and "buy a home on the lake." Then, as we create the retirement plan, that goal becomes one of the markers on the road, and we look for what it would take to get there.

The Appropriate Risks

After that, we find out how much risk the client is willing to accept. We look at scenarios such as what might happen to a couple's portfolio if they are five years into retirement and we hit a 20 percent pullback. It's not that it's going to happen; we're just looking at how that would affect the plan so there are no surprises. What are the effects of inflation? We run that for them. What if interest rates go up? What happens then? Especially on adjustable rate mortgages. I tell people that when they are on a fixed income, they don't want an adjustable rate mortgage. If they were lucky enough to buy that house with a 3 percent mortgage rate, five years from now, that rate could be 7 percent. How are they going to pay for it?

When a new client brings in a portfolio, I ask up front, "Do you know what the risks are in this portfolio? Before I even look at it, could you tell me so I can do some analysis on that?" Most of them don't even know what I'm talking about. They have no idea of the concept of risk.

There are all kinds of software out there that can run the risk model, so your advisor should be able to explain it. If he can't, he's managing that portfolio without a real concept of how much risk he's taking. The advisor may emphasize performance and say, "Let me review your statement to see if I can make it better." He could be peddling his own company's products, or he might just be consulting with Morning Star and creating something that, on paper, beats the statement. An astute investor will say, "That's great but do you understand I'm only at a 60/40 at risk in the market and you just put me at 90 percent? That's not what I wanted." Most people just look at performance. That's why a lot of people's investments go awry. They start moving from one advisor to the other because they think they'll get better performance, only to be frustrated as the market changes.

Money for Now and for Later

I don't ever sell performance. I ask my clients how much money they have and how much they need to live on. Then we talk about how we can get there safely. What's important is that my clients are still living within their means.

Investments reflect needs, wants and tolerances. That's what our programs do. In fact, every morning, we even have alerts showing a list of anything that is out of kilter or showing a major purchase. "What's that for?" I will ask. "Do you understand what it's going to do to your plan?

The aim is to have as little risk as possible, with a targeted rate of return. If the market does go down, which it will, you're not going to get hit as badly. When the market goes up, you won't gain as much, but remember that after a market dip, it takes a far greater return to get back to where you were. If your portfolio cannot tolerate that risk, you need to rethink your exposure to the market. We have various investment models, some more conservative than others, and we tailor a plan to fit your specific needs and goals and ability to deal with risk.

I question clients closely about how soon they will need money and for what purposes. If they tell me they will need money to pay off the house in two years when they retire, we look for a place to park that money, a place that will produce some kind of return. Recently, it has been hard to find such a place. If you buy anything with a two-year duration, you're not even getting 1 percent. In regular times we just buy short-term instruments. If the client tells me he won't need the money for a longer time, then, of course, we can accept more exposure to equities.

Fixed annuities are good for many retirees, with as much as a fourth of the entire portfolio allocated to them. They become a guaranteed way of getting an income. In today's world it's pretty hard to find something that's going to pay consistent income at the rates they are getting. Insurance companies offer avenues to invest differently.

If you have an 8–10-year time frame, then you need a fully diversified portfolio that has a lot of small-cap value—micro caps. Over a 10-year period you'll get more returns off small caps. This is based on the Fama-French studies out of the Chicago school, showing that, over that period of time, small companies turn into large companies, and that is where the premium lies. That's where you make your money.

Now is it volatile? Sure. Over time, you will outperform someone who is overweighted in large-cap stocks. Microsoft is an example of that. In 10 years, its stock has gone nowhere. Apple may be doing the same; it may have reached its peak. What you want to do is find those other companies that are smaller and nimbler, with more profit, and allocate funds to them.

In a 10-year timeframe, even a mix of 75 percent equities and 25 percent fixed income does quite well. It's going to kick out about a 10 percent return over a 20-year period, if you rebalance and do the right thing. That's when you need to say, "That money is set aside and we need to let it grow." I have a lot of those accounts, the "I just don't need it right now" type of account. The model is always liquid and I always can change it.

Clients need to understand the importance of time in the market. Many people get in, have a bad statement, and want out. I say, "You haven't lost any money. Nothing has been sold. Show me the loss. In fact, we should be buying more."

A good, balanced, equities-and-fixed income account is one of the safest things you can have. There are other types of investments including real estate, oil and gas, some of which we are looking at now. More aggressive people can invest in private equity funds that fund small companies and take them public. They are very volatile but the returns are pretty good if you can hang in there. However, you need to understand the risk, and for most retirees, it's not appropriate.

An Investment Model to Fit You

Take a look at the chart on the following page, showing what would have become of a dollar invested 40 years ago in each of our four main models. You can see the progression, and at the end, you will see the percentage of gain and how much money you would have accumulated. You can easily multiply that dollar by whatever amount your initial investment would have been.

Most of the people with whom I am working do not have 40 years before retirement. When I show them this chart and they point out to me that their hair is gray already, I say, "That's not what we're going for here. What I'm showing you is that through a lot of ups and downs in the markets, we have seen everything in 40 years, and investors still came out with a lot more money than when they started.

We have four main portfolios that we mix and match to meet the client's needs. Those four portfolios are audited, and you can see actual returns since 1973. Now, our aggressive model went down in 2008, but it was up, substantially, the year before that and up again, substantially, after that. Our moderate or conservative portfolio only went down 5 percent. Which one can you stand? Which one will let you sleep at night?

Your Biggest Risk of All

If someone walked in here with 5 million dollars, knowing yields were good, and said, "Bill, all I need to live on is $250,000 after tax," I could just ladder a bunch of muni bonds. That's a no-brainer. Now that isn't going to be a lot of growth, but in today's world, you just don't have that. Rates are too low.

Many people do want more juice, but a lot of people would be very happy to live on a few hundred thousand dollars a year tax-free. Perhaps they've gotten to the point where they don't care to grow their portfolio for the sake of growing it. They have enough to do as they enjoy life, and they have concluded that enough is enough. The more money you have, the less risk you have to take if your needs are not exorbitant.

The biggest problem I see is when people walk in here with $500,000 in their retirement account and tell me that they need $50,000 or $60,000 to live on. It's pretty tough. I'm going to really have to go to work to make that happen. We put them into an income-type account and then the first thing they say is, "Well, my account isn't growing that much." Well, if you're taking income from the money being generated, your account won't grow. Dividend-paying stocks don't grow fast as small-cap computer or new technology stocks do. You have to understand and get over the perception that you can make all this money and recover. If you need the income, you need the income.

People get very confused. They'll say, "Well I'm looking at my statement here, and yeah it's creating $70,000 a year in income, but we're only up about 5 or 6 percent from the growth." To which I point out that they also are taking out 5 or 6 percent. Had they left those funds in there, yes, they would be at 10 or 12 percent growth.

That's when they start chasing performance. "Well, I'm going to move over to that guy," a confused client might say. But that guy has no idea. That's the major mistake I see retirees making.

You may notice that's a theme I bring up throughout this book. Some people think investing is child's play. It is, in fact, very complex. You have to practice mind over money and say, "I worked as hard as I could. I accumulated as much as I could, and now this is the lifestyle I can lead if I want to make sure I have enough money for the rest of my years."

If you don't get this under control, if you don't understand how markets work, you are facing your biggest risk of all. You must work with what you have available and nurture it so that it lasts as long as you do. That's the challenge.

Maximum Retirement Spending

Copy of Retire 60 High tax & Infl

Prepared for Luke and Jen Affluent

Depending upon whether you have a surplus or a shortfall, you may be able to change the amount of money you spend annually during retirement. If a surplus exists, you may be able to spend more and still achieve your retirement objectives. If a shortfall exists, reducing the amount you spend could allow you to avoid delaying your retirement.

Retirement is assumed to start in 2017 when Luke is age 60. Retirement for Jen starts in 2024 at age 65. Annual living expenses during retirement are expected to be $180,000 (in today's dollars) and are projected to grow at the specified inflation rate(s) beginning immediately. Desired assets remaining at death are $0.

> Currently, you plan on spending $180,000 (today's dollars) annually after retirement. The most you can spend while still funding your retirement is $130,000 per year.

Under current assumptions, portfolio assets remaining are projected to be ($7,554,308). Using the above result, portfolio assets remaining are projected to be $124,232.

SUMMARY	
Retirement Starts	
Ages 60 & 65	
Living Expenses	
$180,000 (current)	
$130,000 (new)	
Cost of Retirement	
$19,611,494 (current)	
$14,778,092 (new)	
Assets in 2049	
($7,554,308) (current)	
$124,232 (new)	

Portfolio Assets

The chart below shows the amount of portfolio assets you can expect to have in each of the retirement scenarios, one using current assumptions and the other using the above result.

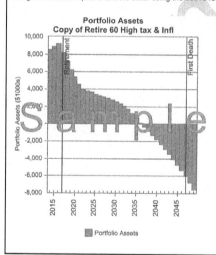

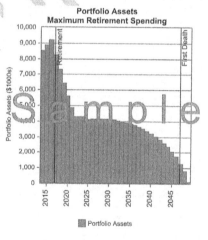

CHAPTER SIX

Threats to Your Wealth

L et this be a warning to investors who are looking merely for performance, and particularly to those who are approaching retirement: There are alligators hiding in the swamp. Watch out. Yes, you do want to make money, but you don't want to put your years of hard work at risk of being gobbled up.

In this chapter I will give an overview of some of those threats that are waiting with jaws wide open. Some of them you have met in earlier chapters. Taxes and inflation are chief among them. We also have talked about market risk itself, and the danger of withdrawing income from an account that fluctuates with the market, particularly if recessionary years come early in your retirement. You face the risk of bond investments losing ground if interest rates rise, as they surely will. You could be at risk from hidden fees in your mutual funds that are sapping your return. A major risk is longevity; you may live longer than your investments are able to support you. And you could face medical and long-term-care needs with the potential to devastate your savings.

Let's take a closer look at some of those threats. If you can identify them, you have a greater chance of avoiding them.

Tax Risk

Taxes can deplete your wealth, even in this tax climate in which rates are relatively low by historical standards. I can remember my dad complaining that he was paying a 90 percent tax. Of course, we had considerably more deductions available in those days, so there was a trade-off.

I pay strict attention to any tax implications when we're trading. I've had clients get upset by their tax situation when they've held a position for a couple of years and it's gone up substantially. One client was invested in Caterpillar. Those shares fell very low and then, after 2009, just took off. They became so overvalued that we took off part of that position. But when the client got his tax bill, he called me about the taxes he had to pay on that sale. I said, "Well, did you expect a write-off? I thought you hired me to make money and not lose money."

Handling taxes is a major area of concern that I review with clients. We look for investments and instruments that will work best for them as taxable, tax-deferred and tax-free assets.

For your taxable investments, the rates on dividends have been low, so even if you're going to pay some on the dividend interest, it's still one of the better places to put your money. Growth stocks that don't pay dividends can be very tax efficient, and that, basically, is what we are looking at. Investments that offer tax deferral are great accumulation devices. Those are your 401(k)s, your retirement plans, even annuities. Because you are excused from paying taxes immediately on your investments, it's like having free money for a while. You're not taking out the taxes on capital gains and short-term gains and dividends. You're reinvesting them back into the portfolio and not worrying about taxation until you decide to take funds out. That can be very lucrative.

The right kind of annuity can be a very good avenue for tax deferral, especially for people with high taxes. I use annuities where I have a very high income client who needs some asset protection, because there is asset protection included in an annuity.

A mistake that I see a lot of people make in retirement, or as they approach retirement, is buying an annuity with tax deferral on the advice of an annuity salesman. Many retirees aren't making the big bucks that they made during their working years. How much tax savings or tax deferral do you really need if you're only in the 15 or 20 percent tax bracket? You're locking your money up, and when you start distributions in, say, four years, the tax rate could be a lot higher than it is today. You could be deferring yourself into a mess. For someone who is paying 38 percent today in taxes, the deferral makes sense. If you're only paying 15 percent, you can actually get yourself into a trap.

As for tax-free assets, municipal bonds work. However, if you're in the wrong city with your bonds, even the ones that are general obligation bonds, they can have some real issues. I always tell people, "If you're going to go to munis, buy the AAAs and try to get them insured." They're not as risk-free as people think. We don't have anything in Detroit in my portfolios or anything in Chicago. You just have to pay attention and not live in what I call a mystical world of safety. All investments have risk.

I've had clients come in with a portfolio entirely of muni bonds. Well, that's been great these last 10 years, but in the next

10 years that may look as bad as if you had treasuries, especially with very long durations or maturity dates. Let's say you have a 3 or 4 percent muni and it's out there 20 years, which a lot of them are, and the 10-year treasury goes back to normal, which is about 4.75 percent. Sure, you will keep getting the tax-free income, but that bond could drop as much as 25 percent in value before it matures. People need to understand that a municipal bond is an investment, and like any other investment, it is subject to losses.

A huge mistake that people make is to pay taxes on money that they just turn around and reinvest.

Some people, for example, don't need the income from their IRAs when they start the required minimum distribution, so instead of spending it, they invest it in something risky, and then they pay taxes again on top of that. It's as if to say, "Well, I paid it once. Now I'm going to pay it three more times."

I always suggest that if you won't need the money for living expenses when you retire, you should invest in a Roth IRA instead of a traditional IRA. That way you pay the tax up front, and the fund will be growing tax-free. In retirement, you will be able to withdraw it without paying additional tax on the gain, and you can leave that money to your children without subjecting them to a tax hit. Otherwise, if you have a traditional IRA or 401(k), the money that you are required to withdraw annually should be used for your living expenses or to pay off debt, or you can just enjoy the money. One tax hit is enough. Don't invite two or three or more. Doing so defeats the purpose of starting a tax deferred program in the first place. It was designed to provide living money. You will always need spending money, so why not use it for that? Meanwhile, you can leave your other investments untouched to grow.

Nonetheless, when clients get their required allotments and don't need it for living, they want me to look for a good way to invest it. They got hit for about 25 percent in taxes when they took the distribution, and now they want me to put that money at risk. In time, that strategy could destroy the net worth they built up.

In Chapter Eight we'll take a closer look at these tax-deferred retirement plans, a major source of tax surprises.

Bond Risk

As I have pointed out, bonds are a highly risky investment at this point in time. If you're in bond mutual funds right now, it's like picking up a dime in front of a steamroller. You'd better be quick. If the Federal Reserve starts to raise interest rates, or they rise by natural market trends, bonds will be in trouble.

We saw this in '94 and '96 when former Federal Reserve Chairman Alan Greenspan was raising rates numerous times within the period of a year and a half. That was very detrimental to bonds, and it will play out again. The market repeats itself, and this time could be worse because we've had such an extended period of low interest rates.

Bonds are like a pendulum. Once they move as low as they can, they don't just come back and settle in the middle. They overshoot and then come back again. Bond mutual funds never recover. If you go down, you'll stay down.

Fees that Reduce Your Investment Return

The fees hiding within mutual funds are another significant factor that influences how much money people have for retirement. Those fees significantly reduce investment returns. The fees are buried deeply in the prospectus, though some regulatory changes would require more disclosure.

When you buy mutual funds, even the ones that you think are no-load, you pay internal fees. You're paying for the transaction cost. You're paying for the brochures and the advertising, and you have to pay the manager. Right now, if you consulted Morningstar and looked at the average fee cost in a growth mutual fund, which has high turnover, it can be as much as 2 percent to 2.5 percent internally.

A lot of clients, when they come to a fee-based advisor, balk at the advisor's fee. Of course, we don't use mutual funds. We use ETFs for individual issues. The cost of an ETF, internally, is about 35 to 45 basis points. If you add that to our 1 percent, you are still paying less than you would with the internal fees of a mutual fund.

People don't understand how those fees sap their investment because they never see them. A prospectus is not exactly light reading, and finding the fees disclosed there is quite a chore. But whether you see them or not, they reduce your return. I call it your bogey: Before you make money, you are paying out about 2.5 percent. That means if the market makes 5 percent, the fees take half of that, so your return is only 2.5 percent. You could have bought a 10-year treasury and done that.

Some mutual fund managers have recently tried to cut their fees, but remember there's a manager to be compensated, and there are marketing costs. Every time you see a commercial for that mutual fund, believe me, it comes out of the investor's pocket.

Inflation and Interest Rate Risk

Inflation is eventually going to come back. Most people should take heed of that. Another major mistake is underestimating how much inflation can cut into a retirement account.

How much do you think the buying power of, say, $1,000 has weakened over 20 years if you have kept that money in your mattress, with no losses or gains? In other words, what would it be worth if you had kept it immune from the market's bears, as well as its bulls?

If you look at the chart here, you will see the "then and now" of various dollar amounts. It demonstrates how much your purchasing dollar is going down in value and inflation is going up. That's why you see the gold bugs around. They have this misperception that if they buy gold, they're going to keep up with inflation. It hasn't ever happened. I'm open to anyone who can show me that it did.

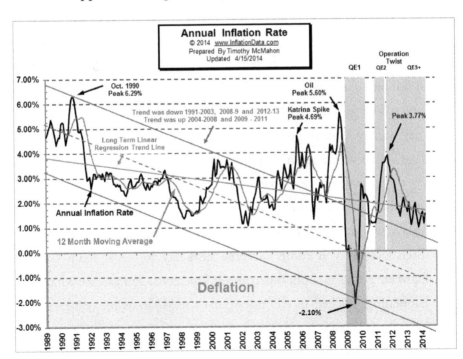

You will see that if you invested in a well-balanced portfolio, you're way ahead. Dividends can be a hedge against inflation. As inflation goes up or business gets better, dividends increase. A lot of companies are raising their dividends. If inflation does return in force, you will have some offset. Dividends can't completely offset inflation, but your money can do a lot better than sitting in a mattress.

You cannot discount the danger that inflation poses to your portfolio. Your investments need to keep up with it. In other words, you run the risk that interest rates will not accommodate your needs.

Take a look, once again, at the bond market. Let's say you have a 10-year bond that you purchased because you were scared the world was coming to an end, and you're getting a 1.75 percent yield. It has a 10-year maturity date. Every time the market goes up 25 basis points, which is 0.25 percent interest rate rise, your bond will drop in value. People don't realize that a full point could cut it in half. That means that if you have a $1,000 bond you want to sell before maturity, you'll only be offered about $500 for it. If buyers can go out and buy bonds at a higher yield, why would they want yours? To get the yield up, you have to take a haircut. That's what will happen with bond mutual funds.

CDs have never kept pace with inflation, ever. The bank is out to make money too. Let's say you go to a bank and buy a CD. In today's world, a five-year CD gets you about a 1.5 percent return. Then let's say you come back the next day for a car loan. Car loans are going at about 6 percent or 7 percent. You can see what's happening. Locked-in CD rates don't rise as fast as interest rates, in general. If rates rise, the bank now quotes you a car loan at, say, 8 percent, but your CD will be paying you the same for five years, unless you want to sell it back to the bank at a discount. People get into that trap.

By contrast, proper portfolio management can bring you more of the upside and less of the downside so that you can better manage inflation and interest rate risk. That, of course, assumes you have enough money to begin with. If your goals are realistic, you have great potential to do well.

I recently did two reviews in Houston. We had pretty good returns. One of the clients was invested 60 percent in equities and 40 percent in bonds. He captured 80 percent of the upside on the market, with a little over half the risk of the market and without being fully invested. The other client was at 50/50, and he captured about 65 percent of the upside. That's all he needed. He said, "I'm very happy getting a 7 percent return at this point in the year. If we stay this way, then by the end of the year, I could be up 12 percent or 14 percent." Under his plan, he needs to make only 7 percent to meet his goals, so the rest is above and beyond.

Health Risks

The biggest deterrent to a successful retirement that I see right now is the prospect of needing long-term care. If you or your spouse becomes disabled or needs to go into a nursing home, the costs can dramatically affect your portfolio. This is one of the major risks that retirees face.

In fact, a sudden need to spend $110,000 a year can destroy a portfolio. Most stays now are about four years. Even if you had a $2 million portfolio when you entered long-term care, within four years your investment potential would have been dealt a powerful blow. The cost of care can take your portfolio down with it.

The risk that medical and long-term-care costs can pose to your portfolio are so significant that I will devote the next chapter to explaining them in more detail with real-life cases in which I have helped people deal with those concerns. Sometimes, in such cases, I was called in early enough to be helpful. At other times, I was called in too late.

The Risk of Yourself

Your own personality could be one of the biggest risks, besides inflation, taxes and a bad manager. There are five to six basic personalities that I see when I interview prospective clients. Let me tell you about some of them. Chances are, at some point, you will think, "That's me."

For example, I recently was working with a woman who had nearly half of her portfolio in the stock of a small oil company where she had worked. The company had gotten in a bit of trouble because of drilling competition. It began cutting its dividends— and she lives off those dividends. But she is so enamored of that stock—she worked there, loves the people—that she will never sell it, despite how volatile it has become. And because she is so heavily invested in it, her whole portfolio suffers.

Her kind of behavior is called "anchoring," and I see it a lot. Some people will feel bonded to an investment, even as other parts off their portfolio far outperform it. But everything comes to an end. Things change. Once upon a time, people might have invested in a company that made buggy whips. If you were invested in such a company today, how might you be doing?

Another personality I see is one of doom and gloom. No matter what you say to such people, their fear of losing money is greater than their desire to make money. I have to coach them through that, saying to them, "You're never going to be able to retire in the lifestyle that you want if you have a constant fear of loss. You have a portfolio that's done very well, historically, so what are you afraid of?"

Then there are those who think they know it all. You see this a lot with professionals, especially doctors, because they have an MD behind their name, or a PhD. It's very hard to get them to put their ego and pride aside. Until they do, however, I don't take them on as clients. They almost have to blow themselves up before they'll come back and sit down and really want to do a financial plan.

Some people have to get to a certain point before they realize that, yes, somebody else knows something. You don't know what you need to know. For example, after Facebook took a hit in its initial public offering—it was priced too high—some clients who had wanted positions in it were pushing to sell the next day. But there is no loss until you take it, and Facebook has a good model that it could monetize. I urged clients to think logically, and now they have profits when they would have had 20 percent losses.

Another personality type is the one who chases performance. Sometimes I'll ask a new client, "How long have you been investing?" He'll tell me and I'll say, "How many different advisors have you had?" If it's more than four, then I have to ask why. Most of the time, that client's relationship with an advisor lasted only for a year or so. The advisor probably put together a pretty good portfolio, but the client decided to take over, didn't know what he was doing, and messed it up.

One client joined us and handed over a couple of million dollars in cash. He got in the market near the end of the year, as it was rising, and it continued to grow the next year. He complained that his return was lagging the market, and I explained that those gains were for people who had invested in the previous fall, not as the market was rising. A good portfolio manager isn't going to try to get in front of the train and get run over. He's going to wait until the train slows down and he can jump on. That gentleman had said he wanted an 8 percent return, and then he saw 12 percent and wondered, "Why am I not getting that?" He had no conception of how markets work.

Performance chasers can get upset and change course. "Well, I want to be aggressive," that client told me, and I had to remind him that wasn't the stance he had wanted previously. "Are you being aggressive," I said, "because you want more performance, or do you want good performance and protection of capital?" An aggressive portfolio, at his age, wouldn't have given him much time to recover if the market went south.

People at times can become their own worst problem. They get out of the market at its bottom, and then they decide to get back in once the market recovers. How does that make sense? And yet their emotions get the best of them.

That's my world: managing people's emotions. I've described some of the more common personality types, and people will see themselves, I'm sure, in those descriptions. Emotions can cloud judgment. Some of the best money managers around are like the old gunfighters, with steel gray eyes.

"The only thing we have to fear is fear itself," Franklin Delano Roosevelt said during his first inaugural address in the depths of the Great Depression. Our worries only worsened the economic tailspin, he was saying. It was time to move forward with confidence, unfettered by negative emotions.

In this chapter, we have looked at some of the major risks out there that retirees face: taxes, inflation, fees, health-care costs and more. But another risk that we face is ourselves. If we don't have a grip on ourselves, we can become a portfolio killer.

CHAPTER SEVEN

Here's to Your Health

"Has anybody you know ever gone into a nursing home?" I often ask clients. "Your mother? Your uncle? Anyone?"

Invariably, they have known someone. "Do you remember the cost?" They nod. And then I ask, "So do we need to talk about long-term care?" The response is usually a strong affirmative from people who have experienced such a situation. However, those who have never been through it tend to procrastinate. Or I hear, "My sister will take care of me," and it turns out that the sister is five years older.

Sometimes they say, "My kids will take care of me." Then when I have a family meeting—which I usually do with my bigger clients—and I explain the financial situation, I'll say, "Kids, the only problem we have here is that if something were to happen, here's how much of the estate will go to nursing home costs." The children ask, "Wait a minute. What can you do about that, Bill?" To that, I say, "Well, you all can buy the long-term care for them and split it up among you. Here's the premium." You wouldn't believe how many of them do that. They don't want to see their inheritance blown away.

Are You Really Able to Pay for Long-Term Care?

If you are highly affluent, you can afford to pay for long-term care, should the need arise. But if you have less than about $5 million, the need for long-term care can be devastating, particularly if it comes in the early years of retirement.

I've had several clients who assumed that they could pay out of pocket if they needed long-term care. They retired in their mid-60s and began spending their money. Then along came a market correction, and their net worth dropped. And that's when they faced a long-term-care need.

One of the clients had built a business with her husband, and they sold it for $4.5 million. I told them that at some point we needed to sit down and talk about long-term care. I ran the analysis for them but could never get them to the table for a serious discussion. A decade into retirement, he had a massive stroke, the sort that once killed people. He lived and developed Alzheimer's disease. She had to begin using her money to pay out of pocket for long-term care, about $750,000 over three years. That left about $2 million. Forty percent of her portfolio was gone. In addition, after the business sale, they had figured they didn't need their life insurance policy anymore, so they let it lapse. Then she had a heart attack and she too had to go into a nursing home.

Eventually, what they left to their three children was only a tenth of what they had planned. I sat down with them for a talk. "Didn't you ever talk to Mom and Dad about long-term care?" one of the daughters asked me. I said I had indeed done so, several times, but they felt the kids would take care of them. People think that's possible, but relatives usually can't provide 24-hour medical care. It was sad. The children had counted on this inheritance, and there wasn't much left. Each got about $150,000. One of them, a successful businessman, gave his portion to the other two.

Afterward, they all came to me to talk about long-term care. It had been an eye-opening experience for them, and that's why I ask people up front if they've known anybody in a long-term-care facility. It's the people who have seen what can happen who want to have a serious discussion. Others live with a false sense of security, figuring it won't be so bad.

Many people resist paying for long-term-care insurance that they may never use. Some of the new products coming out, however, address that concern. They have a death benefit attached so that if you die without going to a long-term-care facility, the money comes back.

If people were disciplined enough to set the money aside in a separate account for long-term care and not touch it, letting it grow moderately, they'd have the money, but nobody does that. It's too easy to get to the money. And it's hard to save that much. In Texas right now the average nursing home is about a $130,000 a year and you have medical costs on top of that.

That's why you will likely need to have $10 million or more before you won't have a need for long-term-care insurance. If you have half that or less, a long-term-care stay can wipe out your dreams. You can be left to feel that you worked all your life just to watch your savings vanish. You can't plan for health-care problems. You can only insure against them.

I tell people I am like a doctor. I can tell them they need to take this medicine, but I can't make them take it every day. I tell people they don't really need the insurance until they are about 55. But the older they get, the more they will pay. And they need to be in good health or the expense for long-term-care insurance goes way up, if it is available at all.

When you are in good health and you think you don't need it, buy it. It does provide peace of mind. That's why few people let these policies lapse once they get them. Most of the ones I use have a death benefit. If you don't need the long-term care, your heirs get the payout. If you do need long-term care, you will be able to afford far better than what you would get in a Medicaid facility. Several of my clients are in a nursing home near my Graham office, and it's as nice as a New York apartment with all the amenities. I compare that to a state-supported home where I've seen some people go. I tell people, sometimes, that if they feel they don't need long-term-care coverage, they should visit both addresses—and then come back and we'll talk.

Do You Need a Medicare Supplement?

Many retirees decide to just take the basic Medicare, figuring they just won't need anything it doesn't cover. And there's a lot it doesn't cover. Dental is not covered by Medicare. Vision is not adequately covered. You no longer will have what you were used to getting under your employer's group benefits or your own health plan.

You need a supplement to take care of things that basic Medicare doesn't. Otherwise, what you pay out of pocket for copays and expenses that are not covered can be as much as $250,000 during 10 or 15 years of retirement. That's without even going into a nursing home or long-term health care, and Medicare is not designed to cover those expenses.

I've had a lot of clients who were caught by surprise. They are healthy when they retire, but then they start having problems, or need dental work, and they discover that Medicare won't foot the bill. It's an added expense that now must be factored in.

That out-of-pocket estimate of $250,000 is going to go up. If you apply average inflation of 3 to 4 percent, over time, that will become $300,000 to $400,000. And, of course, medical inflation is considerably higher than the general inflation rate.

Why People Procrastinate

Many people delay pursuing financial protection for health and long-term-care needs. The cost is the main reason for putting it off. I explain to clients what I'm seeing and review the report with them. Usually, I just advise, but I feel so strongly that they need this protection that sometimes I put on my salesman hat.

They still have trouble justifying the cost. I ask them to look at the potential consequences. Nine out of 10 people cannot save enough to absorb the cost. A couple suddenly has to shell out $120,000 a year, while one of them still has living expenses. I show my clients a graph. It shows how devastating those expenses can be. Within five years, $500,000 to $600,000 is gone. And people are staying longer in long-term care because of the advances of medical science, and so it gets worse.

The Impact On Your Resources

The costs associated with a health event that requires Long Term Care can mount quickly and have a potentially serious impact on your savings. Assets that you expected to have through retirement may need to be liquidated to cover the additional expense of Long Term Care and may become depleted much sooner than they would have otherwise.

Let's assume that **$500,000** of capital resources will be available when **Luke** turns **75**, at which time a need for Long Term Care will arise. Let's also assume these assets will grow at **5.00%** annually, and withdrawals from them will be taxed at **25.0%**.

Your capital resources will be used to offset your Long Term Care costs (**$74,520** per year) as well as your Living Expenses of **$15,000** per month (**$180,000**/year) both of which grow at a rate of **3.00%**.

Without a need for LTC Your resources will last until **2033**
With 4 years of LTC Your resources will last until **2032**
Loss in Years **1**
Loss in Dollars **$534,184**

How quickly will your resources be used?

The chart below shows how the resources available when **Luke** is **75** would be expended. The green area indicates the rate at which the resources are used if no need for Long Term Care arises. The red area shows the same resources being expended in the event that LTC is required. Based on the above assumptions, you can expect a loss of **1 years** of funding which amounts to **$534,184**.

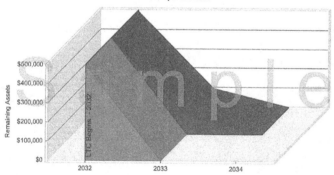

Asset Spend Down

Keep in Mind...

According to the U.S. Census Bureau, the 80+ segment represents the fastest growing segment of the population. With more of the population living longer, there will be more individuals incurring long term care costs. Families need to understand and plan for these costs without expecting them to be covered by government programs or entitlements.

Without protection, there go a couple's dreams. One spouse needs the care, but both of them could sink because the costs of the care are financially debilitating. Or assets that were intended for heirs are sidetracked. For that woman whose husband had a stroke before she herself became ill, I had to get a reverse mortgage on their house, which had been clear of mortgage payments for 15 years. She needed the income supplement. So they would be leaving the kids that much less.

Procrastination often is a matter of denial. I hear many comments such as, "I'm not going to end up like that. If I get sick, I'm just going to die." One guy told me that. But you don't control that. If you have a stroke and need daily care and assistance, you can't really opt out of that. A gentleman in one of my groups has had a series of strokes. A month ago he seemed remarkably healthy for a man of 80. His situation changed suddenly. You will always have worries, but you can mitigate those worries by planning.

And that underscores the importance of planning for the unknown. You need not lie awake worrying.

But Isn't Medicare and Medicaid Enough?

Long-term care, as I write this, is not covered by Obamacare or whatever we end up with. No coverage. The AARP has been trying to get policymakers to consider such coverage, but the insurers have a tough time with this. It's hard for them to come up with a risk profile or analysis on long-term care because it is a moving target. Medical costs keep rising, and people keep living longer. Insurance companies have trouble figuring out how to price such protection so that they don't lose money, particularly on policies with a lifetime benefit. A lot of companies, even large ones, are dropping out of long-term-care coverage. They justify the risk.

The Medicare system is unlikely to be providing coverage, and for the same concerns: the costs involved, and how to set the pricing. It used to be that people would go into a nursing home and would pass away within two years. I have a client who has been in long-term care for seven years. He's 88 years old, and he's still sharp. People have to address these facts. We need to stop thinking of a long-term-care need as something that *might* happen. We need to consider *when* it will happen.

Some people have tried to make themselves indigent on paper by giving their money to their kids or they transfer it, or in one way or another make themselves eligible. It's become harder and harder to do. Right now, the system looks back about three years for any transfer of assets. The problem, again, is procrastination. When someone comes to me and asks how to make such an arrangement—usually, it's the kids who come in with an ailing parent—I refer them to a qualified attorney for advice on transferring assets.

But the clock starts from that point. You have to deal with such a situation early. What happens a lot is that people end up in the nursing home with some assets. They drain those assets, get them down to the point where they can get Medicaid, and then they have to go to some other state-supported type of home.

Long-Term-Care Options

Traditional long-term-care insurance is a reliable option, but you need to acquire it early enough or it will become increasingly difficult to afford.

Alternatively, there are some good products available now that help to address the concern that you never get those premiums back if you never need the care. I used to look down on these insurance and annuity alternatives as smoke and mirrors, but new products are coming out from some of the top-quality insurance companies and I consider them more viable. I'm comfortable with them.

Some of the older products required putting in $200,000. You could take funds out of your IRA and not pay a penalty. You would pay taxes early, prior to age 59½. Then it would be put into an annuity or a life insurance policy to qualify for the care and you would be guaranteed an interest rate on that money. If you put in $200,000, you would be guaranteed $300,000 or $350,000 of benefits for long-term care if needed.

Essentially, as I explained to clients who called to ask me about such offers, that was $200,000 of your own money that you put up to get your own money back. That's not so bad. It gives you peace of mind, and you are investing money for a need that you must address. But it's not like pure insurance. Paying the premium for pure, long-term-care insurance is a lot cheaper than putting down $200,000. That might be 10 years of premiums. And $200,000 of the benefit is your own money. It was a great way to sell an annuity, let's put it that way.

You need to ask the right questions, such as what is the surrender value if you decide not to continue. If you put in $200,000 and want out after three years, what's the haircut? And how is the money invested? Does the rate go up, or is it fixed? Not long ago I saw an offer from a company I had never heard of, for a guaranteed 3 percent, but surrender charges lasted 10 years, starting at 10 percent for the first six years and gradually dropping off after that. And the 3 percent rate was fixed. That was a good deal for the insurance company. Insurance companies can lend money out at a lot more than 3 percent, and to take a 10 percent hit for early surrender is pretty bad. It's an example of smoke and mirrors. Take a close look. What you thought was there simply is not.

Obamacare and Its Effects

How will health-care costs ultimately be affected by the Affordable Care Act? In short, we don't know. There are a lot of unknowns about how it will evolve and whether there will be any coverage for long-term care. I doubt very seriously there will. There are so many uncertainties just with the medical part that it wouldn't seem likely that long-term care would be addressed in the near future.

Clients continue to ask whether Obamacare will cover that need, but I've heard nothing, even from lobbyists, to indicate it has even been brought up. The considerations would be many: How would drugs be administered? How would the doctors be paid, and how would the system get them to participate? How would it work on the insurance exchange?

"Would you rather have a bird in the hand, or two in the bush?" I told one client. Even if Obamacare does eventually provide some coverage, it may not be sufficient. It would just be a supplement. And if it comes at all, it wouldn't be for several years.

Running the Numbers

If you're what I call a mid-level investor who has acquired some assets, anything over about a million dollars up to five or six million, you should definitely sit down with someone knowledgeable and address this concern.

We can run some numbers, do an analysis, and prepare a report. Let's see what the effects would be on your portfolio. Let's estimate an age when you might end up in a long-term-care facility and see what would happen. The key to it is this: If you don't at least talk about it with someone, and you are in complete denial that you will ever need long-term care and believe you can't afford it, then you're putting a lot of people at risk. You are putting an unnecessary burden on your family. Talk about your options and get all the information.

If you don't have protection from the costs of long-term care, you are not only putting your own lifestyle at risk but you are compromising the inheritance you might have hoped you could leave for loved ones. When I prepare an analysis, I advise family members to sit down together and go over the projections. It's not difficult. What's essential is to do it in advance. You can't just show up at an advisor's door when someone goes into a nursing home and expect to do Medicaid planning on the spot.

As always, the amount of risk you accept will be up to you, and if you decide not to have long-term-care protection, you are taking a high-risk position.

CHAPTER EIGHT

The Secret Life of Your 401(k)

The three sisters were mourning the loss of their mother from a heart attack, but they were pleased that Mom had thought about them in her bequests: Each of them was to inherit between $750,000 and a million dollars, and they figured it would be good to set up trust funds for so much money. They were in their 40s or 50s.

They had gone to see a CPA, who referred them to me. It seems all the money was in their mother's IRAs, and she had some large ones, more than she would ever need. When she died, she had been approaching the age when she would be required to take minimum distributions from those deferred-tax accounts.

I looked at each of them across the table, and then I asked them a question, "About these IRAs, did your mom tell you she had set these up as a stretch? Did she say anything like that?" Their answer was what I had feared: "No."

I had to tell them the tax consequences they therefore would face. It's important to understand that if you die with money remaining in your IRA, ordinarily, it will be passed on as a lump sum of taxable income to heirs other than your spouse. The way to avoid that is to set up what is known as a stretch provision, which allows the heir the option of taking distributions over time.

"You all owe about 30 percent in taxes, based on your income levels," I told the sisters. Thirty percent of the portfolio was gone. They weren't too happy, but it had resulted from a lack of planning. "All your mother had to do," I explained, "was to have sat down with someone like me, or a CPA, and say, 'What can I do?'" She didn't expect to die of a heart attack, but it's always important to plan in advance. I tell people, "You start building up assets in an IRA. Sit down and decide how you're going to leave that and stretch it out, because otherwise the tax hit is horrible." We ended up with about $900,000 for each sister, but 30 percent of that went to taxes.

Deferred-tax retirement plans can pose a number of problems. If you withdraw money too soon, you are hit with a penalty, and later, if you fail to take the required distributions, the penalty is huge.

I have had too many clients who lost their job and started living out of their 401(k) at age 55. I had to explain to them that when they take that out, they pay a penalty. The only way to do it is to set up a 72t, which requires withdrawals until age 59½. If the portfolio keeps falling, you still have to take out 5 percent. If you lose 10 percent in the market, you still have to take another 5 percent out.

There's a joke about two guys who graduated from business school at Texas A&M and they wanted to start their own hay-hauling business. They'd go out to the guys who grew the hay, buy a bale for a dollar and then sell it for fifty cents. Well, things weren't working out too well. They went back to their professor and said, "Look at this model. Something is going wrong here." He said, "The only thing I can tell you guys is increase your volume."

That's what happens when people start making these withdrawals out of their 401(k)s or their retirement plans before getting past the penalty clause. Pretty soon, they need to take out even more, and then they take a withdrawal to pay the taxes. They're withdrawing in volume, accelerating their losses. Not a good model.

The Rise of the 401(k)s

The 401(k) contribution plan came into prominence in the early 1980s. They were pretty crude back then, but they did work. Most were investments in group annuities. Of course, interest rates were a lot higher back then; you could do a group annuity and get about 8 percent. These retirement plans evolved out of people's continuing fear that the Social Security system would be running out of money.

They didn't have a lot of bells and whistles, but they were a tax-deferred investment. There were limits on how much could be contributed, but that has gone up as the years have passed. They were seen as a substitute for a defined benefit or a pension plan. Employers turned over responsibility to the investors to plan for retirement.

That's why you see pensions going away. The cost of pensions has much to do with what has happened to Detroit. That's what has happened to Braniff International Airways here in Texas. A lot of struggling companies phased back pensions during those early years, particularly when they were hit by the 1987 crash. So they started getting employees to help plan for their own retirement. There were not a lot of investment choices. The mutual funds often had high commissions. The group annuities were pretty good but basically were in fixed income.

The original cost of those plans also was quite high, with investment and administration fees running as much as 5 percent of the invested dollars. So it was pretty hard for people to make money, especially in the years when the market did not perform that well.

As they matured, they got better. The hope with tax deferral is that Uncle Sam will help you build your retirement plan by putting off the time when the tax will be levied. The idea is that if you put a dollar in, and you are in the 25 percent tax bracket, then Uncle Sam is putting up 25 percent so you can make the most of your investments.

These retirement plans can be a great way to plan, and I am a big advocate of them. If people can be persuaded to invest early enough and are shown how little money they need to invest to secure a good retirement, the results can be amazing.

The Truth about Tax Deferral

In the early days of these plans, the prevailing tax rates were higher, and even with the additional deductions back then, it made sense to defer those taxes. Today's lower tax climate changes that scenario, particularly if you consider that taxes are likely to rise again.

I have clients, especially the ones who work in the aircraft companies around here, who have been at a company for 20 or 30 years and have built up a sizable retirement plan and 401(k). They could be paying more taxes in retirement than they were when they were working.

If you take money from a 401(k) to live on, then that money is taxed as ordinary income. So that's something you have to be careful of when you start planning a 401(k). Try to position your assets so that you wait as long as possible before you have to start taking the required minimum distributions or start using them as an income source.

For those required distributions, the IRS uses a complicated formula. Basically, it works like this. Each year, by Dec. 31, you need to take a distribution of at least 5 percent from your 401(k) plan, or your IRA, or whatever you have converted it to. That withdrawal becomes taxable.

During the recession, some people were having to take early distributions out of their 401(k)s to live on, at a time when their 401(k)s were falling in value. Their required 5 percent withdrawal under the 72t provision of the Internal Revenue Code was using up their money faster than they could make it.

The minimum distributions are a government requirement, but many of my clients don't want the withdrawal. They have enough other income. The tax burden can be pretty heavy on them. In their early years, they might have been in a 20 percent tax bracket, but now they're successful and find themselves in a 35 percent bracket when they are required to take the distribution. The tax deferral didn't quite work out the way it had been projected.

Instead of leaving a bequest to the government, you should do what you can to make sure your heirs get as much as possible of your retirement plan if you die before using all the assets. That's why I emphasize the importance of the stretch provisions that I mentioned earlier in this chapter. If you leave your plan to your spouse, your spouse can keep it going just as if you were alive. But if you leave it to your children, or to another beneficiary other than your spouse, all of it becomes taxable to them as ordinary income in the year that you die.

If that sum is large, then they will be in the highest tax bracket that year and much of the money will be gone. For people who are maxing out their 401(k)s at some of the companies here in Dallas that match dollar for dollar, it doesn't take long to acquire $700,000 or $900,000. For workers in one of the aircraft plants here, employees with 25 or 30 years of service have 401(k) accounts averaging $850,000 in tax-deferred dollars.

That's a big tax hit if your heirs have to take it all at once, and it need not be that way. You often can set up a stretch provision in IRAs that will give your heirs the option of receiving much smaller distributions throughout their lifetime. In effect, the tax deferral function is stretched into the next generation. You have to take the initiative to do that, however.

Roth IRAs and Conversions

Because of the prospect of taxes going up, we have been helping a lot of clients recently to convert their traditional IRA into a

Roth IRA, in which you get the tax break during your retirement instead of when you place the money into the plan. You fund a Roth with money on which you already have paid taxes. When you withdraw your money, it comes to you tax-free.

I'm having a lot of my clients who are in their seventies and aren't having a large income year, start converting over to a Roth. They do so by paying the tax now on the amount of money converted. Taxes are relatively low at the moment, and we can be fairly certain that they will rise. That means the tax break you get later will be more attractive than the tax break you could get now with a traditional IRA. The Roth also takes care of any concern that heirs will be hit with a tax burden, since the money goes to them tax-free as well.

Does conversion to a Roth IRA make sense? It definitely does. It's something you should sit down to discuss with your advisor as you get into your later years. You don't want to do it when you are in your 50s, but once you pass 59½, the age at which you no longer pay the early-withdrawal penalty, I'd say it's something you should incorporate in your plan. We have a special conversion calculator that can help you determine your break-even point—that is, how much you can expect to save in the future, compared with the cost today of doing a conversion.

Most of the time, this is money that the client doesn't need and wants to leave to the children or the grandchildren. Maybe you'd like to set it up for a grandchild's education. The beneficiaries don't pay income tax on a Roth IRA, but it does pass to them as part of your estate and could be subject to estate taxes. Even with the current exemption of $5 million, you will want to watch out for that.

A Call for Caution

To summarize, 401(k)s have become an important tool in retirement planning, but you have to be careful about the investments and the costs. I spend time with my 401(k) participants doing a lot of educational meetings. We teach people how they should be invested to make the most of their plan. Recently, I met with a group of older people and we reviewed investments. Out of fear, some had put their entire portfolio into bond funds. As I write this, in 2013, we're not going to be doing too well on bond funds going forward unless rates stay down for a very long time. People are destroying their portfolios with improper investments. As rates have fallen, bond values have risen, but rates are so low now that they are bound to rise, and the values will fall.

People don't think about that. They flee to a false sense of safety, or they become too aggressive in their investments in hopes of catching up so they will have enough money to retire. The market could do great, as it is doing now. Or we could have another 2008. We had called them 201(k)s back when the tech bubble burst, and in 2008 we were calling them 101(k)s. The risks are all too real.

Sometimes people even copy the investment style of a friend, choosing the same funds. I've seen that a lot. A 55-year-old will think a 35-year-old friend is pretty sharp and will mimic the younger person's choices, even though that person is at a different stage in life.

With some common sense, however, and good advice, you can use a 401(k) to contribute greatly to your retirement dreams. My hope is that you simply become aware of costs involved that might not be readily apparent, and that you plan those distributions carefully for the greatest tax advantage.

CHAPTER NINE

In Your Footprints

One of our clients was going through a very trying divorce and kept putting off my suggestion that he do some estate planning. He just didn't want to get into it at the time. He was building an oil production company. In the interim, we took it public for him and he made several million dollars, which threw us into a whole different estate conversation.

We're in the middle of doing an estate plan for him right now. He's 64 years old and he needs $14 million worth of life insurance to cover the estate taxes for the kids, whom he loves. He had a heart attack three years ago but got over it. It was just a mild one. Still, he went from a smoker to a tobacco chewer, and we are trying to figure out how he can come up with about a million dollars a year to pay the insurance.

This is another investor mistake. A lot could have been talked about. There could have been ways of moving some of these assets into family limited partnerships, and there could have been some charitable deductions, but you have to do that before the fact, not after the fact. Now, he and the kids are asking me what to do because they can see that they would have to liquidate a lot of these oil properties pretty quickly if he were to pass away. He's in good health, but not in the best of health.

To pay a million dollars a year on a policy for 10 years puts an awful strain on someone. That's a major mistake, but similar things happen in all sizes of estate. People procrastinate. They built an enterprise and they want to leave it to the kids, and it's sad to have to say, "If we can't get this straightened out, you guys better be prepared, because you're going to have to come up with about $14 million in estate taxes. That means you have to start liquidating."

Had we done early planning, his insurance would have cost, perhaps, a fourth of the million dollars it will cost now, if we can get it. He needed to have started that process several years earlier.

Dealing with the Inevitable

It's a story that plays out over and over again. Usually, by the time people bring a problem like that to me, it's hard to fix it. They wait until a crisis point triggers them into action.

Estate planning, in essence, involves how your estate will be managed if you become incapacitated or die. By minimizing costs of probate, taxes and fees, you can pass your estate to your loved ones when you want and the way you want. It's not a matter of "if" you will die, but rather, of when you will die. That time is coming, so you must not procrastinate.

Despite talk of lowering the estate tax exemption, in 2013 it was at about $5 million, or $10 million for a married couple.

The possibility that the exemption could be reduced threw a lot of uncertainty into estate planning. However, even as it stands, some people can reach that threshold fairly easily. Everything you own is calculated into it, including the value of your life insurance payout.

Failure to attend to estate planning means your estate is likely to end up in probate for a judge to rule on the distributions. That can be very expensive in a lot of states, such as California. In Florida and here in Texas it's not that expensive, but I still tell people to get it done. It makes the distribution so much easier when that time comes. It's more like a rubber stamp as the judge approves and qualifies the documents. Even if it's just a small estate, you need to have at least a will in place so that it is you, and not the court, who gets to decide where those assets go. And remember that court proceedings are public.

Setting Goals, Keeping Control

Estate planning has a lot to do with goal setting and deciding who and what matters to you. Who are the people and what are the charities and causes that you find meaningful?

The main choice you have is this: You get to decide how to divide your estate, or the state gets to decide. Some people don't care. "Hey, I don't care if the kids have to sell everything to pay the taxes. I'm not buying life insurance." I see some of that. If you are in a second marriage, that adds another twist.

People don't realize the intricacies of dying without some sort of an estate plan, even if it's just a simple will. Your planning needs to be set up to keep the control away from the government. People can show up out of nowhere to lay a claim on your money. That's why your estate needs to be handled by a lawyer of your choosing. You want to maintain your authority to decide what's fair, what's not fair, what's right, and what's not right.

Find someone you trust. If you use an estate planning attorney, make sure that estate planning is indeed his or her specialty. It is quite a complicated area of the law. Before you go see that lawyer, consider the following: Do you have a power of attorney? If not, you will need one. Do you have a will? If so, how long ago was it drawn up? Do you have any trusts? You will want your lawyer to review the documents. Some people have been sold revocable trusts that don't amount to anything. They think they have a trust, but they really have nothing.

A living will and medical power of attorney are also very important, because they grant you control over medical decisions on your behalf if you become incapacitated. If you're in the hospital and you cannot make your own decision on whether to "pull the plug," so to speak, you will want someone as your formal advocate. By deciding in advance the extent of medical heroics that you want the doctors to exercise, you remove the burden of that choice from your loved ones, who will invariably feel conflicted about the right thing to do.

Wills and Trusts

Everyone at least needs a will. That's the minimum. If you have any assets over about $1 million, then you also need to have a trust set up, especially if you want to leave something to your spouse outside the estate.

How do you maintain control over your money after you're gone? A good trust can do that pretty effectively, especially if you have a solid corporate trustee or a bank. You can dictate who gets what, and how much they can have, and when, as if you were still alive. Trusts offer protection from creditors, as well, and they can help to settle matters in divorce cases. However, if you set up the trust without your spouse's knowledge, then some judges will say you did that to circumvent your spouse.

You will want to ensure that those who inherit your money will be good stewards. You need to have a trustee who is credible, knowledgeable and unbiased. You also want to set up provisions for children with special needs. I've done several of those in the last few years. The children had medical issues and the parents or grandparents wanted to set up a trust to make sure the child was given the best of care for a lifetime.

Unfortunately, you also might need to deal with "problem" children. I've seen those in my practice. Some call them "trust fund babies." They're still immature. They don't know how to handle the money because they never had to do so. That is a critical part of drawing up a trust. You can add a variety of controls so that the recipients don't frivolously spend the money. I have seen in my experience that most people inheriting, say, $500,000 to $800,000 will spend almost all of it in about three years if they face no limitations. They've never had so much money, and they spend it frivolously. In a good trust, controls can be set up to make the money last as long as possible. You can add what we call spendthrift clauses. For example, you can regulate how much money can be spent for a car and how often. You can require college graduation before some of the money is released.

I tell young heirs, "Here is the way your dad set up the trust. Here's what he allowed, and here's how much you can get. We're trying to make this last a lifetime instead of five years." They might get upset, but the mandate is clear. And those controls can continue for a long time, usually until age 35 or 40, except for special circumstances—for example, the recipient has a disability or an issue with substance abuse, for example.

In short, a trust can be very flexible. You have a lot of control. It's a continuation of your wishes, as if you were still alive. Setting up a trust correctly requires a professional. Don't use the do-it-yourself online sites. Those might be all right for a simple will, but a trust is complicated, and a lawyer needs to file it with the court and do the proper documentation so that it is valid. Otherwise, you can end up in prolonged legal battles.

Cost of Setting up a Trust

How much it costs to set up a trust depends on the size of the estate, but the costs are not as high as they used to be. Most of the time, estate planning attorneys already have a plan document in which they fill the blanks, making a couple of adjustments here and there. In the old days, they wrote it word for word, but today the body of it is usually preloaded.

The costs I've usually seen range from $1,000 to about $3,000. If they are more than that, then your estate is probably pretty large and money is not an object. The expense is worthwhile. A trust can save a lot of money and heartaches going forward, particularly if there has been a second marriage. You don't want the ex-wife or ex-husband saying, "Wait a minute, what about me?" He or she could get a good attorney and claim you didn't disclose that you had something. You could spend a lot of money on attorney's fees.

The expense of not setting up a trust properly, in other words, can lead you to far greater expenses. The cost of the trust could be, maybe, 10 to 15 percent of what you would spend if you ended up having to go to court.

In helping you to set up a trust, your attorney will need to know about your specific situation, goals and wishes. That's where a good coach or a financial adviser can really help. Most of the time, when my clients consult one or other of the two attorneys we refer them to, they get a better price because I have done a lot of the advance work. I don't charge by the hour; I charge by the asset. When they go in front of the attorney, I've got most of it already worked out. The attorney might suggest a different path, but the legwork is well under way.

Again, teamwork is essential in bringing together the skills of different professionals, with your financial advisor as the quarter-back, or the coach, to coordinate them. I'm not an attorney, but I know attorneys and understand the background work that they need, so I work in concert with them.

Charitable Giving

On larger estates, we often bring charitable giving into play, par-ticularly with estates over $5 million with a variety of trusts. There are numerous methods to set up charitable funds, and they can get pretty complicated, but, in short, your goal is to leave money in the most tax-efficient manner for all involved.

Charitable giving can be a really good way to lower the estate tax, especially if it's done in a timely manner, not the week before you die. It makes you feel good too. If you use Warren Buffett as an example, he basically has pledged to give away about $31 billion to the Gates Foundation to manage for him. That's out of his estate. He has to structure that over time, and there are gift taxes, but there is a deduction for making the charitable contribution.

We talk about that in all of our financial plans when people have what I call excess income or properties that need to be considered for tax efficiency. If they would have to pay large capital gains taxes, they can donate to a charity and circumvent that tax and get the charitable deduction.

The University of Texas has one of the richest endowments around. The last time I heard, 30 to 35 percent of that endowment includes oil wells that owners donated to get them out of their estate. The owners get a deduction for them, and the endowment gets oil wells. We have seen a lot of that. People donate land with appreciated value to get it out of their estate. Otherwise, the heirs could pay taxes on the gain from the original price. The holding is gone from the estate, but the heirs are spared a lot of tax burden.

There are all kinds of ways of setting up such arrangements, and you need a professional to do them. It's not something you want to try on your own. An IRS auditor would ask, "Who drew this up?" If you say it was you, you can call it a checkmate. You just lost.

Estate planning involves issues of insurance and insurance coverage and who gets which accounts, family or charity? Why, for example would you give certain tax-free investments to a charity when the charity is not taxed on what it receives? It all needs to be thought through very carefully. I recently worked with a couple who had joined their separate inheritances with right of survivorship, which could have meant a significant estate tax hit. I referred them to an attorney for a better arrangement.

I also deal with old boys who have been in the oil business for 40 or 50 years, starting out as roughnecks. They got lucky, hit some oil wells, hit some more, and never even looked at how to structure anything. They were just making so much money that they didn't care.

It's time to care. Estate planning lets you be the one who decides who gets the benefits of your life's work. Instead of the government collecting the taxes and distributing them, you know who gets what and you have some say, even long after you're gone.

If you don't have an estate plan, how can you arrange for any continuity of your life's work? If you own a business, are you going to leave it to the oldest son, who has stood by your side, or are all the kids going to come in, including two who never even worked with you? All these things can come up when you're gone if you don't make the decisions up front. I have seen lack of planning pose tremendous problems.

All in the Family

I always suggest bringing the children in together so that the whole family can talk about the overall plan. It doesn't always happen. It depends on the client's attitude. Some of them say, "I don't care what they say, this is how it is going to be." But for families in which everybody is trying to work some things out and they've already had some discussions, these meetings can be valuable. The attorney and CPA can be there as well to explain why we're taking these steps, including strategies to save on taxes. That's really what it's about.

I recently was working with a client who owned a lot of real estate and finally was doing some estate planning. He agreed he would need an insurance policy to cover taxes but added, "Bill, you got to sell it to those three boys, because they're paying for it." He brought them in to see me a week later, telling them, "I want you to listen to this guy. He's got some news for you." I explained the situation. "If you don't have this, here's how much this is going to cost each one of you. For this premium divided by three, I can save you millions of dollars in taxes. The problem is Daddy isn't going to pay for it. You are." And they all did.

Sometimes it does come down to the money. But in a general sense, when people get to this age, they're starting to have deep and long thoughts about what it was all about and what it all meant. That's something you're passing on as well: your values, your ethics, who you were, what you believe, your story, the story of your life. I ask clients what they want to be remembered for. They may reply, "Well, I always loved the Boy Scouts," or "I'm really close to my church," or "I've always tried to help out with the homeless or the needy, so that's what I want to put my name on." As for their business or life's work, they may wish to leave it in the family, but if the kids can't run it, they can't run it. Sometimes I can help with that question, because I get to know the families. They'll ask me, "Who do you think would be the best to run this out of the three boys?" And I'm candid with them. I tell them what I see. Most of the time, they've already seen it.

Some clients just don't want to discuss these matters outright with their kids, so we try a different approach. We have them come down to the office and set up a conference room for a videotaping, in which they explain how they want things handled and who will get what, and why. They lay it all out, and the courts have said this can be admitted if accompanied by a written document. This makes it more personal. It's the parent saying, "Sorry, this is the way I want this done." There are no questions. It can be hard for people to do this, but many have. Nobody sees it until the time of death, and the clients can always review it and change it. We've had a lot of people with troubled families, especially in second marriages, and this approach has worked well for them to establish their final wishes.

Leaving a legacy is not all about money. Passing on personal values is part of the beauty of the video approach. I've had people who have left money to their alma mater or who have dedicated their money to taking care of the homeless. That's part of your legacy. But you have to plan for it. If you don't make provisions, then it isn't going to happen. You can't just wish it. You have to do it.

A Good Night's Sleep

I want you to have a good night's sleep.

My main purpose in writing this book is to give the American investor hope and peace of mind that all is not lost. With some basic planning, assisted by a competent and unbiased advisor, the mistakes that I have pointed out in this book can be eliminated.

This is not a how-to book, which is usually too broad to be effective, and since most investors tend to procrastinate for various reasons, it is best to use an advisor who can make sense of what you need to do and coach you into getting it done.

I can assure you that once you correct the mistakes I have discussed and complete the process, you will find a sense of calm and peace. It feels good to get an important job done. It's like planning for your own funeral. You dread it, but you find that once it is over, you are free from a lot of worry.

People spend more time planning their vacations than they do their financial life, and that is a major reason for the mistakes that I have outlined in this book. The choice you have is this: Do you want to continue in a scarcity mode or in an abundance mode? There are no silver bullets, but you will never get into the abundance mode unless you plan and invest prudently.

Many of my new clients who are approaching retirement or are in retirement are concerned about protecting what they saved all those years that represents a life's work. A good way to do that is to gain insight on what you must not do, and I hope this book has offered such a perspective. You need to find someone who has the training and experience, and whom you can trust, to help you to circumvent the pitfalls of poor planning and bad investing.

It is often said that the definition of insanity is doing the same thing over and over again and expecting a different outcome. Habits are hard to break, especially for investors.

Let me tell you a true story about a man I will call Joe. Joe came to me after losing 78 percent of his portfolio in 2000 because he had chased Internet stocks. We decided that a conservative growth strategy was appropriate, emphasizing *conservative*. Everything was going well until his gambling habit exposed itself again and he demanded that I buy him derivatives, which were paying very high interest. I declined, and he moved the account to a broker who put his entire portfolio into this type of very high-risk instrument to gain about a 3 percent higher yield. The year was 2007.

In 2008 he lost 90 percent of his portfolio. I'm telling you this because Joe was not alone in this type of investing, and some of you probably can relate to Joe's dilemma. Normally, the fault doesn't originate in the portfolio. The problem is the people.

That is why you will find the following words printed on the front door of my office. They represent a twist on a Robert Redford line from *The Horse Whisperer*: "I work on portfolios with people problems."

SUGGESTED READING LIST

Kenneth L. Fisher and Laura Hoffmans, *Markets Never Forget (but People Do): How Your Memory Is Costing You Money—and Why This Time Isn't Different*

Kenneth L. Fisher, Jennifer Chou and Laura Hoffmans, *The Only Three Questions That Still Count: Investing by Knowing What Others Don't*

Ben Graham, *The Intelligent Investor: The Definitive Book on Value Investing, a Book of Practical Counsel*

Jeffrey A. Hirsch, *The Little Book of Stock Market Cycles*

Mark Matson, *Main Street Money: How to Outwit, Outsmart, and Out-Invest Wallstreet's Biggest Bullies*

James Montier, *The Little Book of Behavioral Investing: How Not to Be Your Own Worst Enemy* and *Behavioral Investing: A Practitioners Guide to Applying Behavioral Finance*

Jack D. Schwager, *Market Sense and NonSense: How the Markets Really Work (and How They Don't)*

Steven M. Sears, *The Indomitable Investor: Why a Few Succeed in the Stock Market When Everyone Else Fails*

Jeremy J. Segal, *Stocks for the Long Run*

APPENDIX 1

Chapter One

Retirement Income Industry Association (RIIA), "Benchmarking and Spending Patterns Using the RIIA Retiree Households," and Balance Sheet

RIIA: *Take the Money: Should You Claim Social Security Early?* Webinar by E. Tylor Claggett Jr., Salisbury University

Chapter Two

Index Fund Advisors (IFA), Retirement Plan Analyzer, http://www.ifa.com/retirement-analyzer/

Chapter Three

Dana Anspach, "Five Questions You Should Ask Your Potential Financial Advisor" (see, also, Appendix 3), About.com, "Money over 55," http://moneyover55.about.com/od/findingqualifiedadvisors/a/questionstoask.htm

Chapter Four

Investopedia.com, Four Percent Rule, http://www.investopedia.com/terms/f/four-percent-rule.asp

Chapter Five

maximizemysocialsecurity.com, "When Should I take Social Security to Maximize My Benefits?"

Chapter Six

Denise Appleby, "Roth vs. Traditional IRA: Which Is Right for You?" at Investopedia.com

John Wasik, "Why Mutual Funds Fees Are Outrageously High," http://www.forbes.com/sites/johnwasik/2013/06/27/why-mutual-fund-fees-are-too-high/

Chapter Seven

Nolo Law for All, "Long-Term-Care Insurance: Risk and Benefits," www.nolo.com/

http://www.nolo.com/legal-encyclopedia/long-term-care-insurance-risks-benefits-30043.html

Chapter Eight

Bill Bischoff, "Understanding Taxes on IRA Withdrawals" Market Watch, http://www.marketwatch.com/story/understanding-taxes-on-ira-withdrawals-2014-02-04

Chapter Nine

Constance J. Fontaine, Fundamentals of Estate Planning (Bryn Mawr, Pennsylvania: American College Press, 2010).

APPENDIX 2

The catch-22 questions:

1. What would you like your investments to accomplish?

2. Do you currently have equities in your portfolio?

3. Do you completely understand the stock market?

4. What is your worst investment experience?

5. Do you understand risk and do you know your risk profile number?

6. What is diversification and how do you measure it?

7. Is your current portfolio measuring up to your expectations?

8. Are you paying commission and have you identified your internal cost?

9. Where does your current portfolio fall on the Markowitz efficient frontier?

10. Are you currently working with a financial advisor?

11. Are you familiar with an investment policy statement?

12. Do you have a comprehensive game plan to get you from A to B?

13. How do you determine the success ratio for you current portfolio?

14. Do you know if your current firm participates in any incentives on selling commission products?

15. Do you really comprehend the effects of proper diversification in your portfolio?

16. Does investing make you nervous and anxious?

17. Do you feel you are competent in managing your financial affairs?

18. Do you feel you can work with a financial coach if value added is experienced?

19. Do you have a distribution plan for retirement?

20. Do you know your retirement number?

21. Do you understand the effects of Social Security and health expenses during retirement?

22. Were you able to answer all of these questions with a yes?

These are a few of the questions I ask our prospective clients to answer during our first interview. The reason I call them catch-22 is that if you can't answer all these questions with the proper answers, I would strongly suggest you consult a financial coach.

APPENDIX 3

Five questions to ask a prospective financial advisor:

1. What sort of client is your ideal client?

2. How long have you been practicing as a financial advisor?

3. Can you explain this concept [*fill in the blank*] to me?

4. What assumptions do you use when running retirement planning projections?

5. How are you compensated?

ABOUT THE AUTHOR

William Riley is the chief executive officer and chief compliance officer of Riley Wealth Management, LLC, which he cofounded. He is a 40-year industry veteran, who observed many years ago that, over time, institutional investors typically outperform individual investors while accepting less risk. In his role as CEO, he works tirelessly to make the wealth management strategies used by the world's wealthiest families and largest institutions available to the firm's individual clients.

Riley combines fundamental and technical analysis to minimize investment portfolio risk and maximize potential returns. He uses a variety of noncorrelated asset classes, including alternative investments, to minimize portfolio volatility and facilitate absolute returns in down or flat markets. He believes in a comprehensive approach to wealth management that fully coordinates and seamlessly integrates portfolio management, risk management and asset protection, trust, estate, tax and charitable planning.

Prior to cofounding Riley Wealth Management, Riley held management positions at Merrill Lynch, UBS, Raymond James, Paine Webber and J. C. Bradford. He founded Fort Worth branches for Raymond James and J. C. Bradford.

Before entering the financial services industry, he ran his family's closely held businesses. His experience in operating family businesses, combined with his wealth management experience, makes him uniquely qualified to advise entrepreneurs and business owners on a variety of matters including complex and sensitive issues relating to business succession.

His degrees and designations included a master's degree in business administration, the Chartered Financial Consultant designation (ChFC), the Chartered Life Underwriter designation (CLU) and the Wealth Management Specialist designation (WMS).

A Fort Worth native, Riley is a Texas Christian University alumnus and active in many civic and charitable organizations. He and his wife, Marsha, now reside in Colleyville, and they have four grown children and four grandchildren. When he is not working on portfolios or studying financial markets, he can be found on the golf courses of Ridglea Country Club.

Printed in the USA
CPSIA information can be obtained
at www.ICGtesting.com
JSHW012053140824
68134JS00035B/3405

9 781599 324432